VANISHED
WEST WICKHAM

VANISHED
WEST WICKHAM

Joyce Walker

HOLLIES PUBLICATIONS

Front Cover
Ravenswood   *Bromley Central Library*

Back Cover
Station Road 1994   *Joyce Walker*

Front endpaper
West Wickham c1930

Back endpaper
West Wickham 1994

Other titles from Hollies Publications:
West Wickham — Past into Present
The Long Alert
West Wickham and the Great War
West Wickham in the Second World War

Published by Hollies Publications
69 Hawes Lane, West Wickham, Kent BR4 0DA
First published 1994
© Joyce Walker 1994

ISBN 0 9511655 5 0

Printed and bound in the United Kingdom by
Staples Printers Rochester Limited,
Neptune Close, Medway City Estate, Frindsbury,
Rochester, Kent ME2 4LT

For Christopher, Nicholas and Alexandra

Acknowledgements

The author is indebted to the following for their assistance in the preparation of this book:–

The staff at the Local Studies Department of Bromley Central Library for their patience and cheerful assistance

Bromley Central Library for permission to use copyright photographs

The Centre for Kentish Studies for permission to reproduce a map

Mrs. Mary Daniels for proof-reading

Mrs. Patricia Knowlden for reading the manuscript and making helpful suggestions

The Revd. J. D. B. Poole, the rector of St. John the Baptist church, West Wickham, for allowing me access to church records

Mr. Anthony Raven who read the 'Ravenswood' section and made helpful suggestions

Mrs. Dariel Raven for her generous help with the Wickham College chapter

J. Sainsbury plc for permission to use a copyright photograph

The Estate of the late O. A. Sherrard, and Bodley Head, publishers, for permission to quote extracts from O. A. Sherrard's *Life of Chatham*

Messrs. David, Herbert and John Spencer for access to the Spencer family archives

The staff at West Wickham Library for their help in obtaining books necessary to the project

The following have kindly lent me photographs and documents:–
Mrs. Kathleen Arnott, Mrs. Ida Bennee, Mr. Ivor Davies, Mrs. Mary Hogg, Mrs. Patricia Knowlden, Mrs. Eileen Pitt, Mrs. Dariel Raven, Mrs. Shelagh Rogers and Mr. David Spencer

Contents

Illustrations

Maps

Introduction

Vanished West Wickham began life as the story of a house called Ravenswood and the life and times of some of the people who lived there. Ravenswood was an elegant Queen Anne house that once stood in Station Road (roughly where Boots the Chemists and Sainsbury's are now situated). Then it was decided that *Vanished West Wickham* should embrace other houses in West Wickham that have disappeared in the 20th century, not least because a primary source, common to all but three of the houses in this study, are the diaries of Emily and Ellen Hall, two ladies who lived at Ravenswood from 1842 until their deaths in 1901 and 1911.

The Hall diaries are held in the archives of the Local Studies Department in Bromley Central Library where, provided advance notice is given, they are available for study. Emily's earliest writings have been lost and her surviving diaries begin in 1838 when she was nineteen years of age. Ellen began her diaries in 1838 when she was sixteen years of age and some six months after Victoria came to the throne. There was another sister, Louisa, whose earliest surviving diary dates from 1858, thirteen years after her marriage to James Sherrard, and when she was living at Kinnersley Manor near Reigate. Louisa's entries are mostly of a domestic nature and so do not figure in this book. Emily and Ellen Hall were prolific writers for some 63 years, averaging between them 300,000 words a year, written in large crown octavo books numbering 45 in all. It is to these two ladies that we are indebted for the story of Ravenswood, and for their numerous references to their neighbours in West Wickham from 1842 until 1901, the year in which the final entries in both diaries were made.

The Hall diaries have also been the subject of three books published in the 1960s — *Two Victorian Girls*, *The Halls of Ravenswood* and *Two Victorian Ladies*. The author of *Two Victorian Girls*, Owen Sherrard, died before it was published in 1966, the final version being edited by A. R. Mills, the author of the other two books in the trilogy. These two authors covered almost every aspect of the sisters' lives up to 1869, whether they were travelling abroad or at home; their visits to concerts, art galleries and the like; family visits; their love lives (especially Ellen's);

their views and observations of the wider world around them and, to a lesser extent, the smaller world of West Wickham. It is this smaller world that I have attempted to cover. The results of my researches into the period before and after Emily and Ellen's tenure of Ravenswood are necessarily an adjunct to the Victorian period. It follows too, that because of the amount of 'Ravenswood' material available, the major part of this book is devoted to Ravenswood. Note too that the story of each house is a self-contained account.

Ravenswood

1. *From Grove House to Ravenswood*

Ravenswood was not the only name the old house had borne, for when it was rebuilt in the early 18th century it was known as Grove or Grovelands House. The events leading up to the building of Grove House date back to 1484 when Henry Heydon, Lord of the Manor of West Wickham since 1469, ordered a list of his holdings to be drawn up covering the whole manor, including the area in and around the High Street, then known as Norwood. Each dwelling with its plot of land was identified, as was the tenant and the rent he paid. One of those plots was Groves, home at that time to William Mumford, a yeoman, whose family owned Groves for about 100 years. William Mumford died in 1514 and, perhaps having in mind the comfort and well-being of his descendants, left 20 shillings for the improvement of the highway between the parish church and Langley Green. William's son and heir, John, was named on the West Kent Militia List of 1545 as one of twelve Wickham men ready, armed and fit for service as a billman. (A bill was a kind of long-handled hatchet.) On his death in 1583 John Mumford left four shillings to help maintain the church bells; and Groves to his wife. Then the estimated population of West Wickham, based on rentals, was between 140 and 150.

James Castleford bought the Mumford lands at Norwood, including Groves in c1585. Edward Castleford, one of seven children (at least!) who inherited Groves, mortgaged the property and apparently lost it. In around 1630 Groves was sold to John Huckle.

As well as title deeds and probate inventories, Hearth Tax returns in the 17th century are a helpful source to indicate land holdings and the size of each assessed house. The Hearth Tax was a tax levied between 1662 and 1689 on the number of hearths in every house. Most of the 27 chargeable households in West Wickham between 1662 and 1664 can be given an address, although not the fourteen poorer families living in rented accommodation. In 1664 Groves was occupied by Edward Wooden (sometimes spelled as Wooding) who was required to pay two shillings tax on each of the three hearths in his house, which then, according to Edward's will, consisted of a hall (the principal living-room), a kitchen, and milk-house with a chamber over it. Jane, Edward's

1

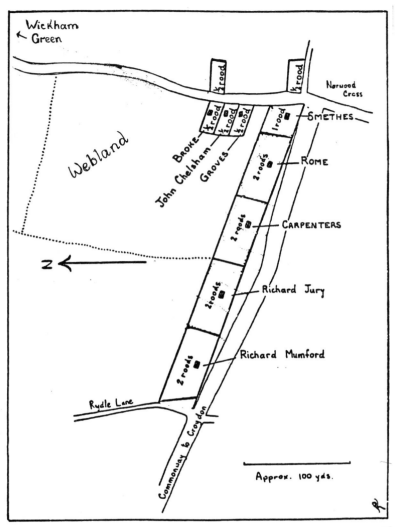

I — Holdings at 'Norwood' 1484   *Patricia Knowlden*

wife, bore eight children including twins who died shortly after birth. Edward Wooden was a churchwarden at the parish church where his name was engraved on a bell hung in 1669. He also took his turn as parish constable (or borsholder as it was known in West Wickham) and as such would have had a whole range of parish responsibilities. Among them would have been the inspection of ale-houses, the maintenance

2

of parish arms, the training of the local militia and the care of the parish bull. When Edward Wooden died in 1677 he was described in his will as a house carpenter but he also farmed 20 acres of land on which he kept horses, cattle, sheep and pigs. A house owned in Beckenham was bequeathed to "my loving wife — all the money she hath in her own custody" plus various household goods and linen.

One of Edward Wooden's descendants, John, was a tenant in 1705 when Thomas Harrison, a London merchant, described in one document as a soapboiler, acquired Groves which was then rebuilt in red brick with dormer windows and renamed Grove or Grovelands House (both names are used in legal documents). The name of Wooden died out in West Wickham when Elizabeth, Edward's great-granddaughter was buried in St. John's churchyard in 1813.

Sometime after 1729 when West Wickham's population had crept to just over 200, Gilbert West and his wife Catherine came to live in Grove House which estate, by this time, stretched from Smethes (now the site of The Swan public house) to Wickham Green, having absorbed Chelsham's and Broke (see Map I). Gilbert West, one of three sons of the Revd. Richard and Mrs. Maria West, was born in 1703 and educated at Eton and Christ Church, Oxford. His two brothers were William, and Temple who became an Admiral and one of the Lords of the Admiralty. There was a sister — Maria (Molly) who lived with Gilbert and his wife for a time. At the age of 54, Molly West married a 31-year-old naval officer, Captain Alex Hood, one day to become a famous Admiral and later created 1st Viscount Bridport. Gilbert's mother was related to the Grenville and Lyttelton families, two of the most powerful families of the day. Gilbert's father, Prebendary of Winchester, died in 1716 when Gilbert was thirteen. His mother afterwards married Sir John Langham.

Gilbert West, while at Oxford, and through the good offices of his uncle, Lord Cobham, served for some time in the Army in 'Cobham's Horse', later known as the 1st (King's) Dragoon Guards. He was afterwards employed by Lord Townshend, the Secretary of State, having been nominated by his university as one of a given number of students to be initiated into the business of state, in order to qualify them for foreign embassies. Gilbert did not advance very far in the diplomatic world because his uncle, who had secured for him Lord Townshend's patronage, became violently opposed to the administration. As a consequence, according to the *Annual Register* of 1782, "Lord Townshend . . . told Mr. West fairly, that he could no longer give support to his acknowledged merit, as his uncle stood in the way of his promotion, and any favour done to him would be construed as a servile court paid to Lord Cobham." Gilbert was compensated with an annual pension of £250 and although not a wealthy man, was able, according to his biographer Dr. Johnson, to devote himself "to learning and to piety" at West Wickham. Catherine West, more preoccupied with domestic affairs, once had to contend with the theft of five holland shirts from the garden. When the case came to court, William Emmett, a local J.P., noted in his diary of 1736 that "Gilbert West occupied a house of Mr. Bartlett's." Catherine's maiden name was Bartlett. Was it that Gilbert's father-in-law had gifted the house as part of a marriage settlement? In 1734 Catherine bore a son named Richard — Gilbert and Catherine's only child.

Gilbert West

Gilbert West became an author and poet. Among his works were *Thoughts on the Resurrection*, *Translations of Pindar* and *The Institution of the Garter*. He also became friend and host to others in the literary world, among

4

them Thomas Gray, Richard Glover and Alexander Pope. James Thorne, in his *Handbook to the Environs of London*, wrote of Glover that he was "subject to strange fits of absence of mind. One morning as Lord Lyttelton looked from his dressing-window he saw Glover in the garden below, pacing to and fro with a whip in his hand and gesticulating vehemently, as though in a fit of poetic ardour. It was in the days when tulips were the rage. Mrs. West was a zealous florist, and she had a bed of choice tulips ready to blow, just then her peculiar care. By these Glover was declaiming, when to his dismay, Lord Lyttelton beheld him suddenly applying his whip vigorously to their stalks and before there was time to waken him from his reverie, the unlucky tulips were levelled to the ground. So entirely unconscious was he that when the devastation was pointed out to him he could with difficulty be brought to believe he had committed it." History does not record Catherine West's reaction.

Grove House also played host to two of Gilbert's friends in the political world — namely, his brother-in-law George Lyttelton and William Pitt the elder. Away from the hustle and bustle of political life they were able to find at Wickham, in Dr. Johnson's words, "books and quiet, a decent table and literary conversation."

In 1747 William Pitt was bequeathed South Lodge at Enfield Chase where, in its 50 acres, he was able to indulge his passion for building and landscape gardening. There too William Pitt was able to provide hospitality to his friends, among them Gilbert. One of those visits was described by Gilbert in a letter to Mrs. Elizabeth Montagu, a leading member of Society and the so-called 'Queen of the Blue Stockings', who was living not far away in Hayes. (Fortunately for posterity the Montagu letters were later published.) "Pitt received and entertained us with great politeness . . . with every mark of friendship and esteem. He had provided for me a wheeling chair [Gilbert suffered from gout] by the help of which I was enabled to visit every sequestered nook, dingle and bosky bower from side to side in that little paradise opened in the wild . . . Kitty [Gilbert's wife] has seemed to be inspired with an unusual flow of spirits, which has not only emboldened her to undertake, but enabled her also to complete the tour, which I was forced to make in my chair, attended by her, Molly and Mr. Pitt."

Elizabeth Montagu had hoped to live in Wickham in a house found for her by Gilbert West, noting that "the pleasure of being near Mr. West gets the better of all my considerations in regard to the situation of my cottage." But later she wrote to her friend Mrs. Boscawen, "The cruel owner of the house near Mr. West makes unreasonable demands, we are going to treat for one about two miles from him [at Hayes] which Mrs. West and he went with me to see yesterday." [15 October 1750] Elizabeth Montagu eventually leased the house at Hayes where she took up residence in 1751. She became great friends with Catherine West and thought that it might be truly said of her "that she always speaks her thought and always thinks the very thing she ought."

Gilbert, affectionately known by his family as 'Tubby', suffered periodically from gout in both hands and feet. Amongst his poems and translations was *Lucian upon the Gout* of which he says in his book of poems, "I translated . . . when I was myself under an attack of that incurable distemper." His sense of humour helped him through many painful episodes as did the support of a loving family. The Wests spent several summers at Tunbridge Wells in the company of Elizabeth Montagu and other notable members of society. Mrs. Montagu wrote to one of her friends, ". . . Mr. West reads to us in the evenings, and the wit of the age supplies us when we do not meet with any in this."

In 1752 the West financial situation improved when William Pitt was able to obtain for Gilbert the lucrative office of one of the clerks extraordinary of the Privy Council. It had helped that Gilbert was a friend of the son of the President of the Council, the Duke of Devonshire. Elizabeth Montagu wrote to Gilbert, "I thank you most heartily for immediately giving me the sincerest joy I have felt for this long time. May you long enjoy what you have so late attained . . ." She did more than offer congratulations, for the following morning she took Gilbert and Catherine with her in her post-chaise to London to stay at her house in Hill Street "so as to be with the President of the Council at 12 o'clock." Gilbert took Mrs. Montagu's advice to go to Court and "kiss hands, a ceremony which upon more deliberation I think it most advisable to go through, however glad I should have been to avoid it."

In the latter part of 1752 Gilbert was busy at Wickham planting his garden with firs and laurels. Elizabeth Montagu wrote to him, "In your garden and in your life, may all that is necessary for shade, for shelter and for comfort be permanent and unchanged. May the pleasures and aromatics be various, successive, sweet and new."

Gilbert, not to be outdone, placed some lines, engraved on a brass plate, in his summerhouse:-

> "Not wrapt in smoky London's sulphurous clouds
> And not far distant, stands my rural cot,
> Neither obnoxious to intruding crowds,
> Nor for the good and friendly too remote.
> And when too much repose brings on the spleen
> Or the gay city's idle pleasure cloy,
> Swift as my changing wish, I change the scene,
> And now the country, now the town enjoy."

While suffering from a severe attack of gout, Gilbert wrote to Elizabeth Montagu on 24 January 1753:

> "The joyous Berenger [a relation on the maternal side to Gilbert West who became Gentleman of the Horse to George III] passed five days with us last week . . . read to us a play in Shakespeare and the 'Volpone' of Dr. Johnson and repeated innumerable scraps out of a hundred others, laughed a great deal, said many droll and witty things and then disappeared, promising to come frequently to strut upon the little stage of Wickham, which you may perceive has been lately graced with almost as great a variety of characters as are exhibited at Drury Lane, so that we have little occasion to run to the great city in search of company, much less for the sake of society."

William Pitt was a fellow sufferer from gout. In May 1753 during an attack which coincided with a bout of depression, Pitt took Gilbert, Catherine and Molly off to Tunbridge Wells where he leased Stone House on Mount Ephraim. Gilbert wrote to Elizabeth Montagu, "I am afraid it will be impossible for me to leave him, as he fancies me of the greatest use to him as a friend and comforter." A week later he wrote, "I think Mr. Pitt is somewhat better, tho' his nights are still sleepless without the aid of opiates." Gilbert was able to leave Pitt for a brief while in the care of William Lyttelton, and return to Wickham, dining with Elizabeth Montagu en route. Pitt did improve and by September was able to travel on to Lord Cobham's great palace at Stowe together with the Wests. It was in September of 1753 that Gilbert took delivery of an urn and wrote to Elizabeth Montagu of ". . . my urn, which is come this very day, and which Mr. Cheer hath taught me to consider as an emblem and monument of the polished, elegant and accomplished Mrs. Montagu, by assuring me that it is indebted for all the extraordinary and highly finished ornaments he hath bestowed upon it, to the great regard and veneration he hath for her, and that will not either for love or money make such another . . . ."

By 1754 William Pitt had within his gift the post of Paymaster General to the Chelsea Hospital, a position which he offered to his friend Gilbert. "The place", wrote Mrs. Montagu, "is called a £1,000 a year . . . and was given with grace that few know how to put into any action . . . they have excellent lodgings annexed to the place. Mr. Pitt dined [with the Wests] on Saturday. What a fine thing it was to act the part of Providence and bless the good."

On 16 November 1754 William Pitt married Hester Grenville, by special licence, in the bride's lodgings in Argyle Street. Gilbert lent Grove House to cousin Hester for the honeymoon while he and his family went to stay with the Archbishop of Canterbury, Dr. Thomas Herring, in his palace at Croydon. Catherine filled the larder at Wickham to overflowing for her guests. Nevertheless Pitt's chef, Mr. Campion, brought in extra supplies and ordered still more to be sent from Croydon, but the honeymoon had to be restricted to ten days because Pitt had to return to the Commons on urgent parliamentary business. The Pitts became very attached to Grove House, no doubt for its memories and the fact that William Pitt had designed a walk there which became known as 'Pitt's Walk'.

When the Commons rose for the Christmas recess, Pitt travelled to Bath leaving his wife behind in their London home. After a few days Hester drove to Wickham to spend Christmas at Grove House where young Richard West was acting host in his parents' absence. The visit proved to be a sad one, for Richard was taken ill and died from what Hester called a bilious fever. Elizabeth Montagu wrote to a friend that she thought the bilious fever "was occasioned by his want of attendance to the jaundice which attacked him in the season of plays and operas, and preferred them to the care of his health. He died very suddenly, the poor parents bear the blow with surprising patience."

It was nearly six months before Gilbert and Catherine could face a return to Wickham, spending some of the intervening period with their friend the Archbishop of Canterbury. Elizabeth Montagu spent a few days with them in June 1755 after which she wrote to Mrs. Boscawen, "Mr. West seemed a good deal affected by his return to Wickham, as to Mrs. West I cannot so well judge, the cheerfulness she puts on is *outré*. Mr. West told me he would alter the room where poor Dick dyed, for he did not like to go into it, and then a soft tender shower fell down his cheeks, he added he had lost much of his relish for Wickham."

Gilbert may have become disaffected with Wickham but William and Hester Pitt were more than happy to stay in his house while they were engaged in buying Mrs. Montagu's house at Hayes after her lease had expired. Owen Sherrard quotes Henry Grenville in his *Life of Chatham* — "London sees nothing of her now and very little of him, except on busy parliamentary days; Wickham possesses them entirely, but they are shortly to remove to their country residence at Hayes . . ."

Gilbert travelled to Tunbridge Wells to recover his health and spirits but neither improved because of a dearth of friends. He wrote to his friend Elizabeth complaining of difficulty in breathing, "accompanied by wheezing", which he thought was asthma. "The Doctors said

8

Hysterical as only fit for *petticoats*" and prescribed asafoetida, valerian and gum ammoniac.

At the end of January 1756 Gilbert returned to Chelsea where, soon after, he suffered a stroke and died two months later on 26 March. He was buried in a vault in St. John's church at Wickham after which his widow went to stay with her sister-in-law, Lady Cobham. Elizabeth Montagu wrote of Catherine to her sister — "She is sensible of her great loss, but says she will behave under her affliction worthy the example of her excellent and worthy husband, and his sentiments of resignation to the will of God, this resolution join'd to natural good spirits and vivacity of mind, supports her in a surprising manner. I wish the good man could have known she would have enjoyed her misfortune so well, apprehensions for her were all that disturbed the peace, I might also say the joy of his deathbed." Catherine West did not enjoy her "misfortune" for long, for she died the following year and was buried in St. John's church beside her husband and son Richard.

Following Catherine's death in 1757, Grove House, then owned by Temple West, was leased to an Irish merchant and banker, Arnold Nesbitt, who also owned the manor of Cricklade in Wiltshire, and was its Member of Parliament. Arnold Nesbitt played his part in West Wickham's parochial affairs, being appointed the local Surveyor of Highways in 1763 and 1764. During Arnold Nesbitt's tenure of Grove House a tax was levied on its 59 windows. This Window Tax had replaced the Hearth Tax and was imposed to help meet the cost of reminting the damaged coin of the realm. Arnold Nesbitt died in 1779.

In 1782 Charles Waller bought the house and its estate, renaming the house Purser's Hall. Three years later he was commissioned into the Royal Regiment of Artillery. In 1818 Charles Waller married Margaret Johnston who bore him three children — Charlotte, Marian, and Charles who followed his father into the Royal Regiment of Artillery. Charles Waller snr. died in 1826, having retired from the Army in 1823 with the rank of Lieutenant Colonel. His son was a Brevet Major when he died at Felixstowe in 1864. However Charles Waller snr. spent relatively little time at Wickham, leasing the house for long periods. Between 1799 and 1805 Grove House/Purser's Hall was leased to William Whitmore. The house soon echoed to the sound of children's voices for William's wife, Eliza, gave birth to three children during that period — John (1799), and twins, Sophia and Charlotte (1801). When the lease of Grove House ran out William Whitmore had the option of renewal but preferred instead to lease an 18th century mansion, Wickham Hall, in Wickham Street (later renamed High Street).

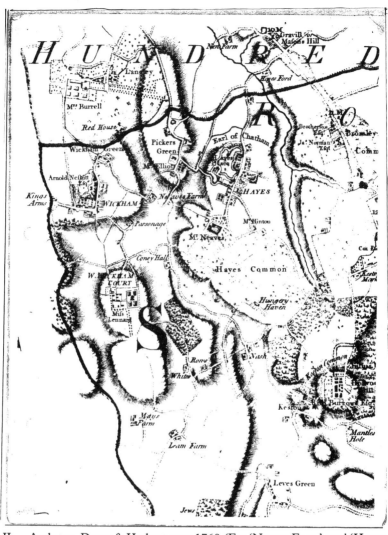

II — Andrews, Drury & Herbert map 1769 (For 'Neaves Farm' read 'Hawes Farm')

Grove House, then still owned by the Waller family, was, in 1805, leased to a leading Swedish diplomat, His Excellency Gothard Mauritz Charles de Rehausen, former Swedish envoy to Portugal who had been transferred to London. His signature appears in West Wickham's Poor-

Rate books so he took some interest in parish affairs. In 1810 diplomatic relations between London and Sweden were severed but Gothard de Rehausen, working mostly from West Wickham, acted as an unofficial representative until normal relations were restored in 1812 when he again served as an envoy, at the same time being appointed a Colonel in the Swedish Army. During the next two years Gothard de Rehausen took part in important political negotiations with Britain including the union of Sweden with Norway. The envoy was created a Baron in 1814 (although he had been styled "Baron" in West Wickham since 1805). Gothard de Rehausen left England in 1817 for Sweden where he died in 1822.

Gothard de Rehausen *Svenska män och kvinnor*

While at Grove House, Gothard's English-born wife, Harriet, already the mother of a son named John, gave birth to four daughters, one of whom, Ida Mary, was baptised in the parish church in 1811. In later years Juliette Lenjonherford, a granddaughter of the Baron, wrote to Ellen Hall in 1897 that one of the Rehausen daughters had died in infancy and, being unbaptised, was buried in the grounds of Grove House and an urn placed over the grave. The medical needs of the de Rehausen family at this time were met by a Bromley doctor, Dr. Ilott

11

Note from Gothard de Rehausen to Dr. Ilott c1811 *Bromley Central Library*
reads — "Baron Rehausen sends the man the Bearer of this to Mr. Ilot requesting
his wound may be dressed; he having gone too near the dog tied up
in the yard, was bit. Should Mr. Ilot be out, B. R. begs Mr. Roberts
would do him the favour to look at the wound which should it require
to be taken care of on the spot, he will pay all expenses of keeping
and curing him . . ."

III — West Wickham & surrounding area 1843

who listed the household in his prescription book:- "Baron de Rehausen, Master, Miss, Mrs., coachman and gardener, housemaid, footman, Mrs. Rehausen's maid, ye Abbe, laundry maid, Miss Ida."

John de Rehausen followed his father into the diplomatic service but succumbed to smallpox in 1854. Although the de Rehausens had left West Wickham in 1817, John chose to be buried at West Wickham where he had spent much of his childhood.

> "Beneath this stone lie the remains of John Gothard
> Baron de Rehausen, envoy extraordinary and minister
> Plenipotentiary of His Majesty the King of Sweden
> and Norway at the Court to St. James. Born in Lisbon
> June 8th 1802. Died in London, March 2nd 1854."

The funeral of the second Baron de Rehausen, Swedish envoy in London at the time of his death, was an impressive affair attended by diplomatic representatives of many countries. The carriages stretched from St. John's church as far as the eye could see.

Following the Baron at Grove House was the Revd. Frederick Gildart, Professor of Civil Law at Cambridge and rector of Spridlington in Lincolnshire. This particular tenant was the subject of village gossip even after his death in 1841. It was said that Frederick Gildart wanted to marry one of his servants, but that Sir Charles Farnaby, then Lord of the Manor of West Wickham, would not countenance such behaviour and arranged a marriage to one of his own kin, Anne Hussey. Anne Gildart died in 1817 aged 42, her husband surviving her for another 24 years. Both Frederick and Anne Gildart are buried in the chancel of St. John's church. In his will, the Revd. Gildart left £75 to the West Wickham Clothing Society; £75 to the West Wickham Shoe Society; £50 for poor persons in West Wickham; one year's wages to each of his servants; and £500 towards the building of a north aisle in St. John's church. Other tangible evidence of his existence is a funeral hatchment hanging in the chancel and another for his wife Anne.

Then in 1842 Charles Hall brought his family to West Wickham and leased Grove House.

2. *The Halls of Ravenswood*

What was Wickham like in 1842 when the Halls took up residence?
The Tithe Commissioners, four years earlier, had remarked on West
Wickham's "contiguity to the Metropolis, [it] abounds with villas and
ornamental grounds of the opulent and the farms, [are] in the hands
of opulent proprietors who have brought the soil into a high state of
cultivation . . . the beauty of the situation and the high cleanliness of
the cultivation render this parish one of the most picturesque in the
Kingdom." The "opulent proprietors" were actually very few in number
since Sir Charles Farnaby, Lord of the Manor, owned three-quarters
of Wickham's 2,600 acres. He was also the rector of the parish church
of St. John the Baptist.

West Wickham, now with a population of 651, boasted a blacksmith,
two bakers, a bricklayer, two coal merchants, a butcher and three grocers.
There were two inns — The Swan and The Wheatsheaf, and at least
three beer-houses — The White Hart, The Leather Bottle and The
Bricklayers Arms. Thomas Cronk ran two daily stage-coaches to The
Ship at Charing Cross from The Swan (four on Sundays). There were
also two daily carriers to London. William Tapsell presided over the
village school, opened in 1818 on Wickham Hill (Corkscrew Hill). Mrs.
Rebecca Jones was a very necessary assistant, since William Tapsell
was also a grocer and letter receiver.

Charles Hall was born in Jamaica in 1783, the third son of William
and Margaret Hall. In 1794 William Hall died and the widow brought
her family to England where the children finished their education.
Charles joined the 16th Light Dragoons, retiring with the rank of Captain
to live comfortably on his private means. He married Augusta Browning
by whom he had five sons and three daughters. The two eldest children,
both boys, died in infancy. Mrs. Augusta Hall died in 1841. By the
time Grove House and its 25-acre estate were leased to Charles Hall,
his three sons — Melmoth, Sydney and Charles — had left the nest.
Melmoth was living in London where he was employed by Child's
Bank; Sydney, also living in London, was a partner in a civil engineering
firm; and Charles was running a sheep farm in Australia. Charles snr.

National School c1900

and his three daughters settled down in West Wickham, christened their new home Ravenswood and the social round began. Calls were made and received, dinner parties were given and attended, and picnics organised. Their attendance at the parish church brought them into contact with the rector, Sir Charles Farnaby. Emily and Ellen's first impressions of him were mixed — "a short squat fat man who reads by no means well, but preaches much better than we expected!" However, some weeks later when the haymakers on the Ravenswood estate threatened to go on strike for higher wages, the rector was praised for his help in a difficult situation.

St. John's church, with the assistance of the Revd. Gildart's legacy, underwent major alterations in 1844 which drew criticism from Emily. She thought that there were too many pews in the north aisle and that the wood should have been stained, not painted in such a light colour. She was not too happy either with the marble slab put up by Admiral West to the members of his family. "Sir Charles called [it] a very handsome one — but his taste is peculiar."

Sydney Hall's partner in the civil engineering firm was James Sherrard who made the acquaintance of Louisa, the eldest of the three Hall sisters. The friendship blossomed, but something went wrong and Papa forbade James the house. It was four years before James and Louisa were able to meet again at Ravenswood. This time the affair prospered

16

and Louisa was married in the parish church on 23 December 1845. Emily described the day.

"There was a crowd of poor people at the church . . . She [Louisa] looked . . . quite lovely. The excitement had flushed her face. George [James' brother] gave her a bouquet of pure white orange flowers and camellias at the door . . . leaning on Papa's arm she walked steadily to the rails and knelt for a moment in private prayer. James placed himself beside her and we all stood around . . . Quietly and in a clear voice my precious sister made all her answers. Firmly and erect she stood before the altar, to join herself to the man she loved . . . At the conclusion as they rose from their knees, James put his arm around her and kissed her through her veil . . . and a more beautiful kiss I never saw — or expect to see. He led her down to the vestry and the registration was made . . . As she walked to the carriage the poor people scattered flowers before her — right up to the steps and some of them put pretty little bouquets into her hands." The wedding breakfast was held at Ravenswood amid a mixture of emotions for Emily, for she was now the head of the household. At three o'clock James and Louisa left to begin their honeymoon.

After the excitement of the wedding Emily and Ellen, chaperoned by their father, went travelling on the Continent. When they arrived home the news was that Sir Charles Farnaby intended to resign as rector at Christmas and that the living was being given to a cousin, John Austen. Emily was moved to write that "we can hardly be worse off and may be much better." In the event the rector did not depart until the following April when he preached his final sermon (later published) making reference to the enlargement of the church, and of the village school opened in 1818 where "the children of the poor . . . have received a sound religious education on the principles of the Established Church." Emily was dismissive. "The good man has done, I doubt not, as well as his lights and not over susceptible conscience permitted."

The girls' expectations of the new incumbent were dashed when Papa's initial report was unfavourable. The Revd. John Austen got off to a bad start too with Emily. "I don't like Mr. Austen — either reading or preaching." Occasionally the family went to St. Mary's at Addington or, in later years, to St. John the Evangelist church at nearby Shirley. Ellen and a friend, Clare Strong, attended the consecration of the Shirley church in July 1856. "The Archbishop was there of course and all the neighbouring clergy. He preached so low we could hardly hear and what we did hear was very dull and little to the purpose."

The village school, where the pupils received their "sound religious education" from the rector, was also favoured with visits from the gentry. Emily described one of her visits — "went to the school and gave the girls a little lesson in geography . . . much pleased to find at the end of an hour that they all said they were not too tired . . ."

Louisa and James returned from their London home to celebrate their first wedding anniversary at Ravenswood. Husband James gave his wife a beautiful turquoise brooch to complete the set of turquoise jewellery he had given her on their wedding day. At dinner, Emily, Ellen, Louisa and Cornelia (Sydney's wife) were dressed all in white. Cornelia and Louisa wore their wedding dresses with camellias in their hair. Cornelia's dress was trimmed with orange flowers and wild roses while Louisa's dress was complemented with her turquoise jewellery. After dinner a silver tankard was passed round "full of some mixture of wine and ale, and very good . . . went round twice, and made some mirth, particularly the doubtful looks of the ladies when they first had the large silver tankard handed to them and the very reluctant way in which they put it down again."

Wickham Court was the manor house and home of Sir Charles Farnaby. In February 1848 Emily and Ellen dined there and met several residents of Bromley, among whom was Mr. Coles Child who had recently purchased Bromley Palace. Mr. Coles Child called at Ravenswood the following Sunday and left his card. Ellen described him as a fine-looking man. Wickham Court was also home to a Book Club — a subscription library. Periodically there were Book Sales and it was at one of these that Emily met the Earl of Devon and his second wife. The Earl's second son, the Revd. Henry Courtenay, lived in Wickham House in Wickham Street opposite The Swan inn.

Emily and Ellen also made the acquaintance of the Shore family who came to live at Elmers End in 1849. Thomas Shore was a clergyman who had refused to subscribe to the Thirty-nine Articles and so could not accept a living. He became a schoolmaster and then a private tutor. Thomas Shore fell in love with Emily despite being 28 years her senior, and a married man. Emily returned his affection, but Papa intervened and put an end to the affair. The friendship was renewed on a purely spiritual level and Thomas became Emily's dearest friend for twenty years, satisfying her need for intellectual conversation.

The Sherrard & Hall engineering firm was suffering from the uncertain economic climate so James and Sydney parted and went their separate ways. Sydney moved to Wales where he founded The Patent Fuel Company, while James became a farmer at Kilboggit near Dublin. In 1850 Sydney, unable to raise £20,000 to keep his firm in business, was loaned shares by his father. This had serious financial repercussions for the Ravenswood household because the dividends were necessary to maintain its standard of living. Not only that, the shares were never returned because Sydney retained them in lieu of a larger share in

Charles Hall's will. Just one year later James Sherrard, who was living largely on capital, borrowed Louisa's trust money from his father-in-law and failed to pay the interest on time, thus compounding the Hall financial difficulties. Charles jnr. was also finding the going tough but solved his problem by selling his Australian wool station for £12,000, sharing the proceeds with his partner.

However, the Hall family was still sufficiently affluent to make a Grand Tour on the Continent, helped in some measure by the letting of Ravenswood for eighteen months. During this Tour Emily and Ellen became concerned about Papa's failing health, rightly so for he died in Naples and was buried there in 1853. The two sisters returned home after thirteen months abroad and went to stay, for the time being, with friends in Jermyn Street in London.

Much to Emily and Ellen's delight, the Crystal Palace, rebuilt from materials from the 1851 Exhibition, was opened in June 1854 in Sydenham, where they soon became regular patrons. A few months

Emily Hall   *Bromley Central Library*   Ellen Hall   *Bromley Central Library*

later there was more cause for delight with the return from Australia of brother Charles who took up residence at Ravenswood. Sisterly love was strained though, when Charles destroyed fruit bushes, ". . . all the old gooseberries and the only quince we have that bore . . ." Emily's relations with Charles were quite often strained, especially when he ridiculed her occasionally professed wish to be employed. A. R. Mills considered that "it was Charles own unemployment that was probably the root of their being out of joint . . . her unquenchable desire to learn . . . Since Charles had returned from Australia he had done nothing . . . coming perilously close to vegetation . . ." Six years later Charles married Emma Geale and Ravenswood reverted to being a place of relative tranquillity for Emily and Ellen who were by now in their middle years, being aged 40 and 38 years respectively.

Emily was moved by the reported sufferings of the wounded soldiers in the Crimean War and wrote to Florence Nightingale offering her services. A reply came from a Miss Stanley on Miss Nightingale's behalf saying "that she would see." However, Ellen was aghast at the idea and persuaded Emily to abandon the notion of nursing in the Crimea. It transpired that ladies were less manageable, women from the lower classes being preferred. Emily swallowed her disappointment and, together with Ellen, prepared about 140 bags of clothing and other necessities for the soldiers — tape, cotton, buttons, scissors, wax, thread, needles etc.

Ravenswood was burgled in 1855. The intruders got in through the larder window and made off with "the little silver spoons used for sugar and tea . . . the Hall clock . . . our worsted wool cushions . . . things of no money value in themselves but very valuable to us — recalling many evenings of tranquil happiness when we worked them as Papa read to us . . . They have taken the hearth rugs old and new . . . they have left us the bear skins and the Opossum rugs — they emptied the caddies of tea — but did not touch either wine or brandy! They cleared the larder entirely — except the great cheese and as ill fortune would have it — we never had before so much meat in the larder — for expecting many friends after all the London visiting is over, I got the meat in to hang it properly. There cannot have been much less than 80lbs of meat, salt and fresh." Emily and Elizabeth, their servant, travelled to Scotland Yard for an interview with a police inspector, but he gave them little cause to hope that their possessions would be recovered. The thieves were never caught.

Ellen, the acknowledged beauty of the family, was a regular patron of the Bromley Balls held in The White Hart Hotel in Bromley. Brother Charles escorted her to a Ball in 1856 and she danced "every dance and refusing three or four gentlemen one after the other. When we first got in, the room was almost half full . . . I took a turn with Charles as we came in in the midst of the first waltz. Then I danced with Mr. Cator of the Peter Cator family. Then a galop with Colonel Cator . . . I ventured to ask Colonel Cator for one [a polka] and he most politely said anything I wished for. So we went to Mr. Bearens and instantly got a polka . . . Arrived at home, really not feeling the least tired, at about 5 o'clock." Next day — "In spite of my twenty-three dances last evening I had slept like a top during my few hours of repose." For the 1858 Ball Ellen wore a new white silk slip, a double skirt of tarlatan with the dress looped up at the sides and a wreath of roses in her hair — white, blush and pink. Her admirers, as ever, were legion.

Aunt Mary, the late Mrs. Hall's sister, died in 1857 and left £7,000 each to Emily and Ellen. The relief is evident in Emily's diary — ". . . we might be able to live a little more comfortably now." They did too, and were able to engage professional singers to entertain at their dinner parties, one of whom was Adelaide Kemble. "Thanks to our singing guest, Miss Kemble, the dinner passed off very well . . . Miss Kemble sang five times — one of them being 'Where the Bee sucks' . . . At the last I [Emily] ventured to ask for something out of the Messiah — which with her powerful voice, is able to give finely — and she complied by singing 'I know that my Redeemer liveth' . . . Miss Kemble kept us up talking cleverly and amusingly — but like her Aunt Fanny she lacks something of refinement . . . She is not handsome at all, and her large wreath worn close upon the forehead and standing high, added most unbecomingly to her already overlong face!" Much later that night, Ellen paid Adelaide Kemble's fee when she "took . . . the £5 note with many thanks to her bedroom."

In December that year Louisa, who was now living at Kinnersley Manor at Sidlow near Reigate, sent her growing family to Ravenswood to avoid contact with an outbreak of scarlet fever among its circle. Geraldine, the seven-year-old, already seriously ill with a brain disease, took a turn for the worse; the nurse in charge was insolent and was discharged on the spot. Then Jane, the Ravenswood cook, suffered an attack of erysipelas but Louisa saved the day by providing her own cook to help out. By Christmas the house was ready to receive its largest gathering for many a year, thanks to Aunt Mary's legacy. The year ended with the baptism in St. John's church of Florence Emily Sherrard, the newest addition to Louisa's brood.

The intermittent procession of Ellen's visiting suitors was one of the features of life at Ravenswood. Emily eventually began to wish heartily that Ellen would marry one of her swains. More acceptable visitors arrived in 1858. Ellen had been "sitting in the stable yard on a log of wood . . . old Crittall [one of the village people] came hobbling into the yard respectfully . . . to know 'if Miss 'Alls would allow him to bring old Admiral West to come and see the 'ouse as his family lived in.' So I shouted into his old ear that we should be very happy at any time to see any of that family etc." Their visitors were two ladies "in deep mourning . . . and an old very gouty gentleman, hobbling along slowly by the help of a thick stick." The old gentleman was Admiral Sir John West, a descendant of the West family who had lived at Ravenswood before the Wallers. The two ladies were the Admiral's daughters who had brought their father to see the grave of Lady Harriet West who had been buried in St. John's churchyard two months previously. One of the ladies described the churchyard as "such a sweet spot, — dear Mama always wanted to be buried here." The "old very gouty gentleman" died four years later aged 87 and was buried beside his wife Harriet.

Past episodes in the history of the house were revived four years later when a Swedish diplomat who "rejoiced in the breakjaw name of Comte Nachmeister, which I cut short to Monsieur le Comte", descended on Ravenswood together with a cousin, the son of Ida de Rehausen. Comte Nachmeister, "pleasing in appearance though plain, with a very gentlemanly manner, was the grandson of the Baron de Rehausen who lived in Wickham from 1805 until 1817. "They said that the Baron took a picture of the place with him to Sweden . . . and they recognised the great Lime, as a little carriage is there represented with the Baron and Baroness in it and some of the daughters . . . They went to see the drawing-room [built by the Baron], the small one having been the Bowery entrance hall . . . and the Hall which the Baron must have used as an Ante-Chamber."

Finding suitable servants was always a problem for Emily — "Spent a day most disagreeably in London hunting for servants." On another occasion she dashed off to Brighton on a very cold October day. "All this bitter cold weather makes us feel it is the real misery to have no servants — but the difficulty of getting these necessary appendages to one's household increases daily . . . It is becoming a social evil. We shall have to invent machines to do servants' work." The Brighton trip produced a maid, Anne Humphreys, "who is as fine as a lady in May Fair and knows nothing whatever but to use a needle." An expedition to Brixton failed to find a gardener.

The rector, John Austen, continued to irritate Emily. At Christmas 1859 the church was still wreathed in black hangings occasioned by Sir Charles Farnaby's death the previous September. Emily thought "that being Christmas the church might have been taken out of mourning." Whatever the rector's apparent shortcomings he was prepared to tell a story against himself which Emily duly wrote down. ". . . his

Revd. John T. Austen and dog   *Bromley Central Library*

little dog was always trying to go to church and always prevented. At
last one morning it got away and appeared in the pew, remained very
quietly seated there all through the service and was wide awake to the
end of the sermon and never tried to go again!"

1860 was a bad year for farmers. A local farmer, William Churcher
of Wickham Court Farm, committed suicide. ". . . he bought two 1 cwt.
weights . . . which he put into each pocket and then jumped from the
deck of a steamer . . . the body never rose to the surface . . . so there
could be no Coroner's inquest."

In 1861 Emily and Ellen bought a house and yard in Wickham Street,
close by Ravenswood. The Croft, as it became known, was a tumbledown
house dating from around 1743. "The yard where the pigs revel, will

be ours in possession next 26 December tho' the price of £1,600 is ridiculously high." They obviously thought the sum worth paying for they were able to plant trees to "be shut out from our neighbours' windows." Emily spoke to 'old Crittall' about The Croft which "we have lately added to the grounds where the Butcher Sheds were, in his youth, the Village cock-pit; 'but in this neighbourhood they were aristotic [sic] and could not make the cocks fight with the usual steel spurs, so they adorned them with silver ones'; which silver spurs he now has . . ."

Three years later the sisters paid £750 for two cottages close by The Croft.

'Old Durling the Forester' was another source for village history. "He says the Elms before this House are hardly any bigger than when he was a boy! Except the end ones, 'which have growed wonderful they have. But Lord Bless You they'll not come down. They'll last your time . . .'"

1861 proved to be a year of acquisitions for Emily and Ellen, the greatest by far being the purchase of Ravenswood from the Waller family for £4,500. They marked the occasion by commissioning the building of a conservatory.

3. *The Halls of Ravenswood*

1861 – 1911

Sir Charles Farnaby's widow, Lady Eliza, died in August 1861 after which time the heir and successor, a nephew Colonel John Cator, took up residence at Wickham Court. He had been required, under the terms of Sir Charles' will, to "take and use the surname of 'Lennard' only and no other surname whatsoever and shall bear the arms and crest of the late Sir Samuel Lennard, either alone or quartered in chief with his own family name." [Lennard was the maiden name of Sir Charles' mother and the family name of the lords of the manor of West Wickham since the late 16th century.] Emily commented, "Never did any one come to good prosperity with less goodwill and wishes of his neighbours . . . Report declares that Colonel Cator dismissed all the servants before she [Lady Farnaby] had been a few hours dead . . ." He incurred Emily and Ellen's wrath with his stated intentions of fencing in the oaks on the Common where the sisters had so often delighted in summer picnics. Thereafter Colonel Cator/Lennard could do no right in the Hall sisters' eyes.

A request from the rector to lease the Ravenswood kitchen garden for a site for a separate infants' school was turned down. Mr. Lewis Loyd, a local landowner, came to the rescue by donating a plot of land at the west end of Wickham Street, almost opposite The Wheatsheaf.

The foundation stone of the school was laid on a very hot 5 October 1861. Emily and Ellen "found good Mr. Austen standing on a plank in the middle of the hole dug for the foundations and all the little children gathered behind him . . . He made a little speech, good man, during which he acquitted himself with glory as he did not blunder more than every sixth word and got to the end at last. Then the children sang 'God Save the Queen' and Mr. Austen said a few sentences very appropriate, from the Psalms and a few prayers. All this time the masons were, as Ellen said, perspiring dreadfully under the weight of the great block of stone. Then Howden spread the mortar very neatly and with a little silver trowel little Ellen Cator . . . terribly shy and frightened, was helped to put a little dab under the block and the least of the little Steuarts did the same, and [it] was lowered into place and a spirit level used to see that it lay even . . . if the trees could remain intact it would be an ornament to the village."

The Infants School, built to the design of "John Adam, lately dead at Bath", had to be paid for and so a bazaar in aid of the building fund was held in the main school (now Greenhayes) on Wickham Hill. The bazaar was rather a squeeze, or as Emily put it, "a desperate cram", the ladies' hooped dresses not helping the situation. The poor people were admitted free on the second day of the sale and were invited to take part in 1d. and ½d. raffles "which enchanted the people and produced better prices than would have been at first expected, besides clearing off all the rubbish."

During one of the sisters' trips abroad, Flora the dog was entrusted to the care of Thorne the coachman. Unfortunately Flora went missing so Emily deducted one shilling a week from the coachman's wages to pay for the missing dog. Thorne promptly issued a summons in the County Court where it was stated that during Thorne's employment at Ravenswood four dogs had gone missing — "valuable terriers of the Pepper and Mustard breed." Emily found the court experience quite daunting, especially when she "had to walk right across the great room, every one staring at the lady whose coachman had summoned her into Court." Emily won the case but lost her coachman.

Emily and her sister were becoming disenchanted with West Wickham, their feelings heightened by talk of a railway coming through the village. "No one wants it . . . What money would pay us for the extreme discomfort of having navvies swarming over the place . . . and the crowd of villas and all the rest of it . . ." There was talk of "making a new Railway from Beckenham to Croydon! It would have . . . to pass through Wickham to Elmers End . . . a frightful nuisance . . . the neighbourhood is changing woefully for the worse . . . the changes are so many and so great that . . . one's inducements to remain here are proving fewer and fewer."

A year later in 1862 — "It is a horrible fact that a railway is actually projected thro' this village . . . No one wants it and many of us village landholders detest it . . . Mr. Austen showed us some . . . of its route. Right thro' Langley Park and our cottages which we have been repairing and building all this Summer . . . It proposed to go through poor Mr. Austen's rick yard, out of the corner of his Terrace and raise an Embankment! 46′ high across our pretty valley right opposite his windows! However it is not yet settled . . ." There was even talk of possibly three lines running either through or near West Wickham including a direct track to Brighton.

An agent from the railway company, Mr. Figers, "called by appointment. Ellen says I tried his civility sorely — I did not mean it.

But the idea of cutting up all our pretty country simply to gratify the covetous money lending greed of such men as Col. Lennard and others . . . makes me so angry that I find it difficult to speak about it . . ." Happily for Emily news arrived in June that the Railway Bill had been thrown out. It was not until 1882 that a line running from Elmers End through West Wickham to Hayes would be opened.

One of the outings in the vicinity took Emily and Ellen via "South End and Bromley, coming home by Hayes. Went in amongst the Hop fields there . . . Men are setting Hops in hopes of having better success with them this year than for two or three previous years." The two sisters attended school ceremonies, both locally and in outlying villages. "Went in the afternoon to Ballards to a school-feast . . . the schoolchildren enjoyed themselves immensely, jumping in sacks. One absurd race among the upper classes made us all laugh. Each was given a wooden spoon in the flat bowl of which was an egg! and the game is to run, if you can . . . self and spoon with its contents to the winning post . . ."

On other visits, to Wickham Court, Emily and Ellen by now in their 40s, observed and recorded the changes made to the manor house. In September 1864 — "The outside has been altered somewhat by the addition of a chimney which has been built with the little battlements which poor Sir Charles had the vile taste to put on the towers. One would be delighted if Colonel Cator would restore the extinguisher tops which once covered the four towers . . . Colonel Lennard, as I

Wickham Court 1930

must learn to call him, took us out to show how he has had to cut away the ivy . . . discovered some pretty little old quatrefoil lights . . . All the rooms have oak ceilings which have been plastered up!" In 1868 — "Instead of entering in the North we now drive into a sort of courtyard in the East . . . We were shown in by a side passage into a very grand room with a parquet floor . . . This is the new wing — and runs at a right angle with the old house almost to the kitchen garden. The dear old dining and drawing rooms all pulled to pieces to be made into one drawing-room and doing this they have discovered a tracery over the door — looking like an old short window . . . The Hall is being made a Billiards room — they have left the old staircase untouched and built another for the new part . . . one regrets that there can be no law passed preventing free will and liberty of action in architects and their employers so that the few remains of antiquity we still possess might be preserved to us." [Emily would be delighted to know that Wickham Court is now a Grade 1 listed building.] Further visits recorded in Emily's diary noted the loss of the bow window from the drawing-room and that the mantelpiece in the new billiards room had revealed itself, after being stripped of paint, as being made of oak inlaid with ebony.

The standard of music at the parish church was a continual source of wonderment to both Emily and Ellen. They had seen the demise of the barrel organ and the introduction of a harmonium with Robert

18th century Wickham Court with "extinguisher tops"

28

The Swan and Elm House

Harman acting both as organist and choirmaster. Robert Harman was also the village carrier who, according to Emily had "picked up his musics literally on the road, going with the cart to and from London . . . very creditable to him, but hardly sufficient for playing an organ and teaching a choir to sing" — a comment made after a subscription list was raised to pay for a new pipe organ in the parish church. Evidently others agreed for Harman was replaced a few months later.

In 1864, as part of their plans for improving the Ravenswood estate, Emily and Ellen sought permission from the vestry to make a new road with a footpath to replace the narrow dark pathless lane that ran by Ravenswood. Colonel Lennard was not in favour of the plan and succeeded in having the proposals rejected, much to the sisters' annoyance. The vestry minutes record that "the said plan does not offer to the public sufficient benefit to induce the vestry to agree to it." It was to be many years before what was to be Station Road came into being.

William Crittall, landlord of The Swan, gave up his lease in 1864 and moved to Elm House just a few yards away. William Crittall's mother was delighted to leave The Swan "and in no ways finds it dull . . . She is to be seen sitting in the parlour, dressed in her best with a nice widow's cap on and the news paper in her hands. She sits close to the window without a piece of blind!" William McDaniel, the new landlord of The Swan, leased two fields on the Ravenswood estate for

29

his cattle. Time and time again the cattle strayed into the grounds of Ravenswood, much to the evident irritation of Emily and Ellen.

At much the same time the forge, almost opposite Ravenswood, was added to the Ravenswood estate at a cost of £700 but the estate was not only being enlarged but also beautified. Saturday 1 October 1864 — "Yesterday some trees came to be planted and we all went out to see where they should go. The Acacia and the Cypress were planted in The Croft and the Wellingtonia close to the Ice House . . ."

The Forge c1867

Monthly Penny Readings were introduced by the rector. They were held in the village school on Wickham Hill where Emily and Ellen became regular patrons. Ellen described the one held in February 1867 when the "children were allowed to behave badly while Mr. Neville showed off some dissolving views and sang some pretty songs in a rather vulgar manner — and at the end a most insufferably vulgar one which had much better not have been sung at all, all about a pretty 'servant maid of Paddington Green'", The *Bromley Record* reported that the "dissolving views were of 'Scenes in the Holy Land', 'The Ascent of Mont Blanc', 'Robinson Crusoe' and the amusing 'Tale of a Tub'."

While Emily and Ellen were travelling in Europe during the winter of 1866 severe gales wreaked havoc among the trees in West Wickham. "In some of the hedgerows by Wickham Court they have gone down

30

like ninepins . . . and our dear old mulberry." One of their acquaintances, William Thomas, told the sisters that "some parks looked as if they had been cut down as a mower cuts down grass."

More upset was caused when "poor wretched Jane", who had worked at Ravenswood since 1842, was discovered drunk in the wine cellar. ". . . she could not stand, but leaned against the door which she had opened by getting the key out of our key box . . . her candle shook in her hand, and she could not speak." After a further lapse Jane was dismissed. There must have been something about Ravenswood's wine cellar for Nancy, Jane's successor, was found there with a lad, named Brett, from the nearby Swan public house. "She is a giddy flighty girl who has got her head full of lover's nonsense."

The burning down of Croydon parish church in 1867 was mourned by the sisters — attributed by them to the over-heating of the flues. Fire was still on their minds when "the man came to see after our Hot Water apparatus. His Father did all the Stove part of the Crystal Palace . . . He always told the Managers that unless an alteration was made there would some day be a fire! This caution was neglected and the destruction of the most most beautiful and most attractive part of the Palace . . ." — a reference to the fire at Crystal Palace in December 1866 which destroyed the tropical section.

Wickham Hall, a house in Wickham Street, came on to the market in 1867. William Cator the owner offered it to the tenant, William Dickenson, who was unable to raise the necessary capital to finance the asking price of £20,000 for the house and its 68-acre estate. Emily sought advice from Lewis Loyd who advised her to buy as much land adjoining Ravenswood as she could afford. It was rumoured, correctly as it happened, that Mr. James Forbes, General Manager of the London, Chatham & Dover Railway, "was sweet upon the house." He bought, at the subsequent auction in 1868, the house and a 12-acre field for the sum of £8,250. Emily's bid of £3,315 for the 12-acre Lodge Field was accepted. This field had a public footpath running over it which Emily and Ellen wanted "to turn a little . . ." They consulted Mr. Latter of Bromley who advised them to "'make the new path easy and let the old one become uneasy and it will soon turn itself' . . . and we are going to follow his advice." That was not the end of the story of Lodge Field.

Emily suggests in her diary that other bids were made on her behalf for the entire property. ". . . we should probably have had great difficulties in managing so large a place and the house and must have gone abroad if all had fallen to us. I ought to be glad perhaps that it is as it is — Mr. Forbes will live there and not build and as we have now kept the speculators off from our vicinity we have got all that was really needful but of course I should have been better pleased to have *all* the block . . ." Emily was not doing too badly for when the *Returns of Owners of Land* was published in 1873 Emily was shown as owning 52 acres compared with 30 acres in 1859.

The summer of 1868 was a very hot and dry one with prayers said in churches for rain. There was a fire at Wickham Court Farm where Emily and Ellen inspected the damage. "By some incomprehensible want of forethought they allowed the Forge to have its opening into the straw yard so just after dinner as they were shoeing a horse, a spark flew off from the shoe . . . right into a mass of loose straw lying for litter. This dry weather and the hot sun had made it all like a lucifer match. The pigs were all destroyed to the number of 45. Two valuable cows and a colt six weeks old . . . were got out unhurt." Valuable farm machinery was destroyed but fortunately the wind changed and took the flames away from stacks of corn. Even more fortunately Mr. Taylor the farmer had not long before doubled his insurance.

One of the visitors to Ravenswood that summer was Mrs. Dinah Craik, the novelist, who declared that she and her husband liked the neighbourhood so much that they intended building a house on a plot of land they had bought at Shortlands. Norman Shaw was to be the architect, who was later to be engaged by Emily and Ellen to design a library for Ravenswood.

Then came news, which outraged Emily and Ellen, that Colonel Lennard had succeeded in his plans to build houses on Wickham Common. Sixteen acres were set aside for two houses — "the poles run up and many of the beautiful thorn trees go as well as the public path! The railings will come close to the beautiful oaks that we have so often delighted in sketching."

The plans for a new library at Ravenswood having been approved, the work was well in hand by May 1870. Norman Shaw was very busy in the neighbourhood, for not only was he building the Craik house at Shortlands and supervising the alterations to Ravenswood, but he was also remodelling Wickham House in Wickham Street.

The alterations at Ravenswood required that an upstairs room be converted into a passage to the new room, "the Library or the Attic — or whatever it will be called", which would be 37 feet in length. Emily wrote in her diary of "Mr. Shaw being most amiable and does not laugh at us for changeableness of mind." Fateful words indeed. Emily elected to have plain wood, "my own doing — the glass I have left to Mr. Shaw — on whose shoulders the praise or the blame must rest." So there the matter rested and the two sisters went travelling on the Continent while the work proceeded.

Emily's diary entry of 7 December 1870 splutters over the page. "The new room has been *painted*! I am perfectly furious at Mr. Shaw . . . all the woodwork has been daubed over with this detestable white paint . . . He makes me dislike the whole addition — glaring, ghastly, odious, chalkey abomination — where I wanted only the simple wood — I was very angry with Mr. Shaw for his most impertinent, and I may say, insolent letter about the money — but really this painting is beyond endurance — I hardly know what to do or say — However it shall all be taken off and let him say what he will . . . The inside is all unfinished — filled with scaffolding — and the windows with glass such as I hate — all yellow and green, instead of being pure and colourless. In short I am disgusted and extremely angry and regret that we trusted anything to him . . . and then he talks of our not having any confidence in him!" A few days later — "Mr. Shaw and I are likely to come to fisty cuffs . . . has more than usual Scotch determination to be always in the right tho' it is against the whole world. I was a fool not to have anything written down . . ." Ellen was equally appalled — "clearly it was a great mistake having no contract and trusting Mr. Shaw as though he were a gentleman . . ." Eventually a compromise was reached. Norman Shaw agreed to remove the paint inside the house while Emily, for her part, agreed to wait a few months before reaching a decision on the exterior paintwork. Ellen was more philosophical — "we shall doubtless come to like it."

Simpson's, the builders, shocked Emily and Ellen by submitting a bill for £996. They though it should have been in the region of £650 and so passed the bill on to Norman Shaw who succeeded in getting it reduced to £800. Ellen was indignant, "he engaged that the building, all included, should be a little over £600 . . . I think that we are imposed upon between the Architect and builder. But I suppose we shall have to pay it." Charles Harrison, their adviser, did what he could and tried to delay payment but Simpson's demanded an immediate payment of £150 and threatened to charge interest on the remainder if it were delayed. It would seem that the matter dragged on, for Robert Shaw's Abstract of his father's accounts includes a receipt, in 1873, from "Miss Hall Ravenswood West Wickham for £48.12s.6d."

Living in close proximity to The Swan sometimes posed problems for the Hall sisters. ". . . a night or two ago men were fighting there — with a terrible din and bleeding like stuck pigs. The servant had to take the letters to the post . . . She handed them over to the butcher's boy for which Ellen reproved her, whereupon she returned to see if they were safe. The men were still there but their quarrelling tipsiness had changed into the affectionate form and one of them desired to testify his appreciation of the servant's charms in a way that had no charms

for her, and she returned very red with anger and broke out at once —
she had never been so insulted in all her life — and her eyes flashed '.
. . one of them drunken fellows tried to kiss me! However he got a
good smack on his face for his pains . . ."

The Swan 1881   *Bromley Central Library*

Harvest Festivals were celebrated by church services and Harvest
Homes for the labourers. They were a blend of solemnity and jollity,
always beginning with a procession to St. John's church, consisting of
a band leading the farmers and their employees, and all wearing
distinguishing rosettes. The service of thanksgiving was followed by a
meal served to the farm-workers in either a barn or a marquee. At tea-
time it was the turn of the women and children to be entertained. Dancing
and games were then the order of the day. In 1873 Emily and Ellen
waited at the lychgate "where all the gentry gathered together to watch
the labourers and tenants, headed by Colonel Lennard and Mr. Taylor
with bouquets of oats and poppies (very pretty), preceded by a most
discordant band of music, with banners flying — which drew up on
either side of the gate — played them into church . . . all the big boys
of the village . . . having some indication of the day in bundles of corn
and autumn flowers . . . They all bowed, except Tidy . . . Mrs. Lennard
goodnaturedly gave up her seat and went with her boy into one of the
open sittings while she made room for us. The service was a great deal

too long — the whole service with extra thanksgiving prayers . . . many hymns and that blessed Canon Austen preaching a long sermon . . . brought itself to an end at last and we got out. Some went with the farmers into the tent and the others accompanied Mrs. Lennard to lunch. The meal was satisfactory and pleasant . . . I had Miss Bonham Carter and Mrs. William Cator on either side of me . . . When the men, 150 of them, got in, Mr. Dyke [the curate] standing at the end of the tables, called out loudly 'you will all stand up and take off your hats' and then said grace and all the guests fell to helping the men to beef and plum pudding. The Lennard girls trotted about with the plates and Mr. Taylor and Mr. Goodhart and Colonel Lennard and the others cut up the meat fast and furious — so did the eating — one man . . . had his plate filled four times — at least! It was a sight to see Captain Torrens with his arms full of plates, acting butler as if to the manner born."

Itinerant labourers were used to help bring in the harvest. Emily spoke to some reapers "who mow instead of the old-fashioned and much more picturesque work with the sickle. They are London men, out they said, on their work for a 'lark', having little or nothing else at this season . . . in dark winter times as gas burners, which is warm and pleasant, but for a change — 'the country well ono' and very pretty'. They made a pretty picture themselves having lighted a fire near a huge Elm tree and set up a kettle on their sticks tripod fashion. They are paid 15/- an acre."

Emily felt strongly about the emancipation of women and the difficulties to be encountered, "almost as great as if they were veritable slaves instead of being only the slaves of custom . . . If it were possible to raise women to give them self-respect . . . we should raise our men, for though it is true that the men make the women what they are, it is much more true that women make men what we see them . . . But oh the mischief that the clamorous, writing, angry social science women are doing! I cannot bear to think of them — they are like Traitors in our Camp." Emily fretted too about what she described as "the low moral tone of our working-classes, especially as it seems in an agricultural district and the impossibility of raising it. So long as landlords let their houses be like pigsties . . . with this the fearful degradation of so great a number of women . . . I could weep my eyes out for the abasement and degradation of my sisterhood."

The position of women in society continued to exercise Emily's pen — "Tuesday November 1872. Went to London to attend a meeting at the Adelphi on the subject of Women's Education and for the first time heard women speaking in public . . . Miss Emily Davies, principal of Girton College, spoke well and easily . . . Mrs. Grey made an admirable speech." When a branch of the National Society for Women's Suffrage was formed in Beckenham in 1882, both Emily and Ellen enrolled and became enthusiastic supporters of the movement.

Emily paid a visit to Thomas Walton's cottage at Wickham Green. "Looked in on Walton's thatched cottage — is one of the few remaining specimens of the 'good old days' in this village. It is a fairly picturesque black outside. Inside those 'merrie days' . . . are well represented by the utter misery and squalor, dampness and darkness which reigns tho' the woman is a hard working creature enough . . . Crittall is the landlord — one suited to the good old times — his cottages represent the worst. He won't do anything to them . . . so the floor is below the level of the road, paved with bricks broken and sunk, the windows 2′ x 1′, glazed with small panes, and low doors — the chimney a cavern up which one can look to the sky . . . a disgrace to any village."

Painting of cottages at Wickham Green   *John Danby*

36

Since 1869 the landscape painter, John Collinson Danby (sometimes known as Collinson Danby or Jacob C. Danby), "tall, pale and sickly looking", and his mother had lodged in a cottage at Wickham Green owned by Emily and Ellen. There he made sketches of other cottages including Thomas Walton's thatched cottage. John Danby was subsequently to exhibit at the Royal Society of British Artists, and the British Institution, despite Emily's opinion that "no one can make him aware of his deficiencies. He insisted on giving me his sketch of the inside of Walton's pigsty cottage." John Danby fell on hard times and in 1883 attempted suicide by drinking carbolic acid. He was found in time and recovered after treatment. Since suicide was a criminal offence, John Danby was duly charged at the Chislehurst Petty Sessions, where, after evidence was given concerning his circumstances and the fact that several gentlemen in West Wickham were prepared to dispose of his paintings for John Danby's benefit, he was discharged. He left the cottage at Wickham Green for which he had paid no rent for three years and moved to a cottage at Nash owned by Sir John Lennard (knighted in 1880). John Danby died, a pauper, in Bromley Union Infirmary in 1912 and was buried in St. John's churchyard.

Soldiers marching through West Wickham on their way to various barracks were not an unfamiliar sight. Much to Emily's delight the 3rd Dragoon Guards, en route from Maidstone to Croydon, came through the village in July 1873 together with their band — "the officers coming last, Colonel Tower in a Cocked Hat and Crimean medals and two others. It was impossible to imagine anything prettier then the red coats looked, winding among the trees, as we saw them at the four cross-roads."

In December 1873 Emily and Ellen visited North Africa, found it to their liking and bought a house in Algiers. They were to spend several winters there. On their outward journeys their railway director friend, James Forbes, arranged for the Express to Dover to stop at Beckenham Station especially for them. Emily called it a "pleasant arrangement". On another occasion in November 1893 a guard on the train from Charing Cross to Elmers End provided Ellen with a foot warmer. A porter at Elmers End then transferred the foot warmer to a carriage on the train to West Wickham where John Ridge, the station-master, took charge of it, refilling it with hot water for the return journey. Another pleasant arrangement.

The sisters arrived home after the winter of 1874 spent in Algiers, to find that the rector, John Austen, was in failing health. He died in 1876 and was succeeded by Ythil Barrington. Not a few eyebrows were raised when Colonel Lennard failed to attend John Austen's funeral, electing instead to go racing at Ascot!

Wickham Hill c1900

The gift of the living was in the hands of the Lord of the Manor, and was given usually to a relative or friend of the Lennards, but on this occasion, it having been declined by Colonel Lennard's brother, the Revd. William Cator, William was invited to find a replacement. Village gossip had it that the Revd. Barrington came to West Wickham as a result of an advertisement in *The Guardian*! Emily discovered the truth from the rector's wife herself. "She tells me that they [visited] Paris several years ago and were asked by friends to call on the Cators, and liked them . . . As if struck by sudden inspiration he enquired would Mr. Barrington accept a benefice if offered one? To the affirmative he made immediate reply. Then you must come down to Carshalton tomorrow and we will talk the matter over. They drove down accordingly the next day and there Mr. Cator unfolded to them this idea that this living was vacant and that he had best see it and think of it . . ."

Emily described Ythil Barrington as "a rather tall large man with a beard . . . a loud voice. He reads clearly but rapidly . . . not badly but not specially well and moves quickly." She also noted the changes made in the services at the parish church including the "unusual step of announcing the marriages to be from the communion rails . . . he churched a woman in the *middle* of the service." However Ythil Barrington earned Emily's approbation with "his sermon . . . just 11 minutes" and the fact that the rector was "very highly connected — Lord Darnley, as well as Lord Barrington being a cousin . . . and the Bishop of Norwich is his uncle."

The new rector was unable to take up immediate residence at the rectory because it was in a state of disrepair and so lodgings were found for him in Wickham Street. Soon after Ythil Barrington began his ministry he made use of the Infants School as his 'Mission House' as it was dubbed, where both Emily and Ellen attended the evening services. They approved of his "capital sermons" and, remembering John Austen's lengthy Harvest Thanksgiving services, were delighted that the new rector, by the expedient of moving the Harvest Service forward to 12.30 pm, was able to use the shorter evening prayers. (Two years later the school was converted to a church dedicated to St. Augustine, to a design of an amateur architect, J. St. Aubyn, the cost of £1,000 being borne by Lewis Loyd.) The two sisters were delighted too when the rector and his wife joined them on the committee of the local branch of the women's suffrage movement. The rector was also instrumental in providing a Lecture Hall in Sussex Road in 1878.

Interior of St. Augustine's church

There was a fire in April 1875 in the Ravenswood stables. The *Bromley Record* reported that "immediately on its discovery, plenty of help was forthcoming and it was got under before it spread to the adjoining premises. The Bromley Fire Brigade, under the direction of Mr. J. Dunn, was on the spot 40 minutes after receiving the alarm, but the

Beckenham Brigade was unfortunately unable to exhibit quite so much promptness."

Emily and Ellen sometimes made use of a rather special stage coach run by Charles Hoare Esq. of Kelsey Manor, Beckenham. The 'Rapide" Coach, as it was known, ran from The Swan to Charing Cross. "On Wednesday [19 September 1877] we went to The Swan to take the coach . . . all the way to London. They passed the gates exactly at 9 o'clock and we were inside and off within 5′. The guard saw after us, Mr. Hoare coming out of The Swan to mount on the box and drive off after a formal bow to us . . . We went at a good pace and in 15′ we were at Beckenham, changing horses at The George . . . After leaving Dulwich . . . arrived at the bridge at 10.30. Soon afterwards the guard asked us where we would alight and Charlie Hoare coming up to the window said he was about to leave the coach but that his man would take us to any place we wished for on the road to Piccadilly."

The Goodhart family owned land in West Wickham, and Langley Park in Beckenham. Langley Park was in a somewhat neglected state following the illness of the then owner, Charles Goodhart. Emily took a friend for a walk in the grounds and found the "Bath House — a beautiful place originally — with a large swimming place under cover and another outside, a lined tank and clear water but the flooring tiles are displaced and broken. The ivy is growing thro' the roof and the roots of the trees are heaving up the pavement and in a few years it will be all a ruin if nothing is done."

Ravenswood and its grounds were given over to the Red Lion Street Sunday School outing in the summer of 1878 when 600 children from Clerkenwell descended on West Wickham in seventeen buses, "living, breathing, rejoicing little souls waving handkerchiefs and screaming at the tops of their voices. The boys were all marched down the Nut Walk — the girls down Pitt's Walk, . . . but alas there . . . the Program was shipwrecked . . . the swings — 6 of them in sight and away went the foremost boys pell mell — jumping and clambering over the hurdles. The confusion was sent down the ranks and all were rushing helter and skelter to the great attraction, the girls straying all over the lawn . . . After lunch, donkey rides, Aunt Sallies for cocoanuts, drives in Costermongers' carts, races and swinging went on at a great rate. Frank and I made a diversion by races at the end of Burrell's Meads, where the winner had a donkey ride . . . 30 went off under the escort of a very big boy to a walk to Hayes Common . . . At last races and prize giving came to an end and they ate and drank beyond a sufficiency and Lady Dacre supplemented the meal with a huge bag of Brandy Balls." Thanks were expressed by the teachers who made a presentation of a Morocco bound Bible to James Sherrard, the organiser of the event. "James was delighted and poor Louisa, as James said of her, 'enjoyed herself thoroughly, she was crying the whole time', and then after much cheering and applause James returned thanks and another cheer was raised as the baskets of flowers were brought out. Ellen and I gave them, aided by the [Forbes] girls and Frank, who handed them to us as fast as we distributed them, and the teachers then marched them all down to the vans . . . They were loaded up without difficulty — but as usual, sundry and divers were interlopey waifs and strays, good for nothings I fear, who had come uninvited." There were problems with the drivers who were reluctant to carry more than they had been paid for — "'cos ma'am it aint no ways fair, that it aint. We bus-topped vans have to take all these, and more than they canvas-topped — they are paid just the same as we bus-topped' . . . somehow it was stilled and away the 17 vans all went at last, the children, in spite of the pounds of bread and butter and cake and tea, all cheering and waving flags and handkerchiefs and making as much riot as at their arrival."

Emily ended the day tired but thankful that it had gone well. She wrote a postscript to her diary entry for that day — "I provided some huge tubs of water and made many of the dirtiest children wash faces and hands. They found it so agreeable that I believe I should have offered it as a prize! for a race! They washed and washed and soused their heads in! coming up like ducks to breathe and shaking the water from their eyes. 'Oh that is nice!' Poor things, they can seldom have unlimited supplies in their miserable courts."

On 30 May 1882 the first train steamed into West Wickham. Emily and Ellen missed this momentous occasion for they had let Ravenswood for two years to a leather factor, William Brooksbank, and were residing in Algiers. It was a deliriously happy day for local children because travel was free on that first day and many of them made countless journeys between Elmers End and Hayes. The Railway Hotel, financed and built by Nalder & Colyer the Croydon brewers, opened in 1882. It had been suggested that refreshment rooms be provided at the Station but the brewers rejected that idea. The nearby Leather Bottle, once a beer-house, but at the time of its purchase by the railway company in 1880, a private house, was, together with four adjoining cottages, used for housing railway employees. By this time Pig (sometimes known as Pix) Park was entirely built over — Kent, Surrey, Sussex and North Roads coming into being. Emily regretted that she and Ellen had been unable to buy Pig Park now "covered with cottages and drains. The district is becoming a nuisance to the gentry. The people have all, save the last house . . . joined in filling up *our* ditch — men going the length of building their sheds round our trees . . . a village midwife constantly engaged among the poor people there." Emily had a point. Between

1881 and 1891 the population of West Wickham rose from 963 to 1,262.

Kent Road late 19th century

More alterations were made to Ravenswood when, in late 1883 George Dumbrell, a local bricklayer, was commissioned to make a cellar under the servants' hall, at the same time replacing the stone floor with a wooden one. An old larder was made into a bathroom.

Ythil Barrington had been appointed rector for a term of eight years and so had to leave West Wickham in 1884. He had proved to be, after a few hiccups, a well-liked minister and was showered with farewell gifts including 100 guineas, a silver salver, a walking-stick set in silver, and an album of photographs of West Wickham.

42

After one of Emily and Ellen's sojourns in Algiers they returned home to find that a cousin of the Lennards had been appointed the new rector. He was Harry Bertie Roberts who, much to the sisters' dismay, had introduced several changes in the services in the parish church. The choir had been brought down from the gallery, clad in surplices and seated in pews beside the organ. "They make as much of a procession as the limited church room admits to and go . . . past our pew, down by the Font and to their seats beside the Organ." Emily was shocked to hear the psalms chanted as well as the responses to the prayers. The rector caused more consternation by moving around the church during the service and allowing flowers and lighted candles to be placed on the communion table. Emily was convinced that the congregation would be "gradually led on the green pastures of incense and embroidered vestments and confession . . ."

Lodge Field, a field on the Ravenswood estate, became a regular bone of contention between the sisters and the "big boys and drunken men" who regularly tore down the fencing so that they could harry the cows and even play cricket there, calling it 'The Recreation Ground'. The rector tried to mediate, suggesting that Lodge Field be let out for a public playground, a suggestion that was rejected out of hand. While Emily and Ellen were living in Algiers they continued in their efforts to block the public right of way through the field to the railway station. Trigg, the gardener, was constantly replacing and repairing the barbed-wire fencing despite Mr. Latter's warning of possible litigation for damage caused to clothing. Emily thought she had found a satisfactory solution when Charles Creed, landlord of The Railway Hotel, rented the field for his cattle, at the same time undertaking to keep the fencing in good repair. "He will manage, I hope, to prevent the very troublesome Pig Parkites from flinging broken bottles, old hardware and suchlike rubbish onto the field." Soon afterwards on 4 November 1890, Emily received a letter from the Bromley Highways Board — "'The attention of this authority has been called to the enclosure of a footpath at West Wickham over land of which you are the owner . . . in its present state is likely to prove highly dangerous to the Public . . .' So we are to remove the fence which has cost us £70 to put up . . . The field has been rampaged over by all who like . . . The police are no more use than a rope of sand. They say they watch but nothing is done."

Almost inevitably Emily faced litigation. In 1891 she was sued by Mrs. Sophia Neville for injuries sustained when she fell over the stile erected on the right of way through Lodge Field. Emily lost the case and had to pay £30 damages and costs.

Having been cast as the villain in the court case, Emily was later to be praised for her help in securing what remained of West Wickham

Common. The Common was originally 75 acres in extent, but Sir John Lennard enclosed some 50 acres of the Common and sold them for building development. The *Beckenham Journal* of 3 May 1890 reported that "a tall iron railing spiked and close set, is being run up . . . began three weeks ago . . . There are those who hold that the lord of the manor, Sir John Lennard, is enclosing what does not belong to him . . . all who love the country should insist on having the question of rights cleared up . . ." The campaign to save the Common was spearheaded by the Bromley District Commons and Footpath Preservation Society which sought to find a commoner who had common rights and who would fight to keep the Common open.

The *Beckenham Journal* of 27 February 1892 gave an account of a public meeting held in the Bromley Grand Hall, under the auspices of the Preservation Society. The chairman spoke of "the exertions of Mr. Birkett, the solicitor to the Society, . . . had discovered an old copyhold enfranchisement, and in that the right of the commoner was upheld." That commoner turned out to be Emily Hall who had not only been able to produce the relevant title deed, but also one of her father's old account books containing an entry in 1843 relating to gravel having been cut from the pit on the Common and "carted over to Wickham by Crittall's men." As a result of this discovery, Sir John Lennard had, the *Beckenham Journal* went on, "been wise enough to come down from the position he had thereto maintained and offered to sell the existing portion for £2,000 and to surrender all his rights to the public for ever." A public subscription raised £1,500, the remaining £500 being provided by the Corporation of the City of London which also agreed to administer the Common. Emily was unashamedly gleeful at having scored over her old adversary, "to find himself opposed by a couple of those despised and poor women . . ."

The Lord Mayor of London travelled to West Wickham Common in November 1892 to declare the Common free and open to the use of the public in perpetuity. The "despised and poor women" were among the guests invited to take part in the procession from Bromley Station to West Wickham Common, and the subsequent proceedings. On the appointed day Emily and Ellen, accompanied by their niece Edith Sherrard, drove to Bromley Station to meet the Lord Mayor who had travelled from London in a special train. Their friend, Mr. Ritherden, a leading campaigner in the fight to save the Common, directed them to their places outside the Station. Ellen gave up her place in the coach procession to Edith. "At least half an hour late the Lord Mayor appeared — but before his arrival we had seen the carriages and servants go past, first rather scrubby and then in all their magnificentness — with wigs and three-cornered hats and turned-up hats with feather edging — the lamps filled with flowers — the servants with enormous bouquets to match and flowers on the horses' heads. . ."

There was a celebratory banquet in the evening at The Albion Tavern in London attended by both the outgoing and incoming Lord Mayors. Ladies were barred from the evening festivities and so James Sherrard was invited as a representative of both Emily and Ellen. "The dinner he enjoyed greatly. It was extremely handsome and excellent."

One battle Emily and Ellen did lose was with the rector and churchwardens at the parish church. St. John's church had had its seating rearranged, losing all the rented pews in the process. The sisters were furious that their pew had disappeared and Ellen expressed her feelings quite forcefully in a letter to the rector. He replied saying that "as a clergyman he felt it was better I should take no notice . . ." Bertie (as he was known) Roberts wrote also to Emily stating that he had obtained permission of the archdeacon and that the parishioners had no right to any pew. What was even more galling was that the rearrangement of the interior of the church had been the work of one of their tenants, John Sedding. However, when surplus pews were disposed of, Emily was very pleased with Killicks the builders, who used some of the wood for a high dado in the passages leading to the Ravenswood kitchens. This was not the only instance of surplus timber being used at Ravenswood. Soon after the library had been built in 1870, the hall was panelled using oak from Bromley College Chapel. When Lady Caroline Legge, a regular visitor, called at Ravenswood at the time when the hall was being made ready "she instantly spied the inscription in gold letters to the benevolent Miss Shepherd [sic — probably the Mrs. Sheppard who gave £12,000 for Sheppard College] who gave an endowment to the College — it puzzled her so much that Em was forced to explain."

Emily was again in trouble with the authorities in 1895 over the stile and right of way through to the railway station. The newly established West Wickham Parish Council considered the matter. The report of its Sanitary Committee was highly critical. It said that "the obnoxious and still dangerous stile should be removed . . . Another York slabstone might be added to the one existing in order to prevent people stepping into the ditch, several accidents having occurred there . . . the disgraceful state of the public path compels people to take the longer road round The Swan . . . The wire fence running from above the post . . . is made unnecessarily of barbed wire . . . We propose that the barbed wire should be removed."

In the latter part of the 19th century, because of "our administrator's dishonest action in Algiers" Emily and Ellen were forced to let Ravenswood and live abroad for long periods in their house in Algiers, but in 1897 they were able to return to "our dear old home . . . so green and delightful. One had almost forgotten how beautiful the trees are!" Ellen explained to Mrs. Goodhart how much cheaper it was to live in Algiers where "the whole style of living is so much simpler and less costly than here. For instance, in Algiers we have two servants in the house and two outside — here living in the quiet way we do — we have four inside and three men outside."

Sometime during this period Emily and Ellen received a visit from Louisa's married son Charles (affectionately known as 'Willie') and his son Owen. Many years later Owen was to recall in the preface to his *Life of Chatham* "my father taking me to visit two spinster great-aunts . . . Their house . . . was full of charm and dignity . . . The elder, whom I met first, seemed to me — and I believe was — extremely formidable, and her presence crushed me into a depressed silence. The younger, when she entered, proved to be of a very different cast. In her youth she had been dazzling and in old age still retained the gentleness of beauty without its arrogance. She noticed my gloom and suggested that I should be happier playing in the garden until it was time for tea, and as she pushed me through the door, recommended Pitt Walk as the ideal playground . . . overhung by tall trees. It was shut in on each side by thick evergreens, and it ran with undeviating decision to nowhere in particular."

Emily had suffered from severe headaches and deafness since her 30s and in later years rheumatism was to afflict her severely. This meant that Ellen, despite her own increasing deafness, was forced to take over the running of the household. Emily's use of the pen remained undiminished — "It is a painful fact, but I am steadily-improving for the worse . . . I crept to the little church fairly well. Returning had to lean against a garden door — too spent to move." She agreed to try electrical treatment for her rheumatism. This was in 1899 when she was 80 years of age. "The two doctors to work their will on my 'corpus vile' — the pins and needles like Dr. Nissens — a sort of harmonising making me start continually, but not paining, the nerves being excited. One produces the current, Dr. Craig applies it . . ." The second treatment — "Doctors gave me a great dose of lightning. It is quite innocent in results as far as I can discover . . . looking back a few months I am worse than I was . . . I am of the opinion that they are profoundly ignorant or their electricity is nothing but poking about in the dark . . ."

Emily and Ellen spent their last winter in Algiers in late 1899. On their return to England Emily's condition worsened and attendance at church was only possible with the help of a bath-chair. Emily was more concerned about Queen Victoria's failing health and when it became apparent in January 1901 that the Queen was dying, she wrote

46

"How can we live without her . . . She is the life of our Land." Emily's final sentence in her diary, written on 26 January 1901, referred to the Royal Funeral. "The whole ceremonial wanted nothing to make all that was fitting for the interment of a sovereign so great and beloved as ours."

Ellen wrote on 2 April 1901, "Dearest Emily is able to talk to me very little generally because using my tube tries her, but she did begin to look over her journals and talk over everything." On 13 April — "Yesterday my dearest Emily seemed more ill, weak and weary . . ." Two weeks later Emily died and was buried in St. John's churchyard.

There was still the matter of the footpath across Ravenswood land. The West Wickham Parish Council urged the Bromley Rural District Council to write to Ellen asking her to honour an agreement to put the footpath in order. Joseph Killick, one of the parish councillors, visited Ellen and gave her an estimate for the work. At Ellen's request he also undertook to lop the trees on the Ravenswood estate that were causing a nuisance.

Aside from the offending footpath many of the villagers were taking a keen interest in the Boer War which , when over, was marked by the presentation of silver matchboxes to local serving men. The *Bromley Record* in May 1902, reported the welcome given to Lieutenant Packe,

West Wickham Brass Band *Bromley Central Library*

"recently returned . . . and on his arrival at West Wickham the inhabitants gave him a most hearty welcome home. The horses were taken out of the carriage, ropes were affixed to it, and headed by the West Wickham Brass Band, the men pulled the carriage home in Triumph to Hawes Down . . ."

The trees on the Ravenswood estate continued to cause problems and their care was entrusted to Joseph Durling, the parish clerk. In 1908, 58-year-old Robert Dunmall, of Pickhurst Green while working as a sub-contractor for Joseph Durling, slipped and fell from a height of between 50 and 60 feet and later died in Beckenham Cottage Hospital from his injuries. As a consequence of the accident Ellen was sued in Bromley County Court by the widow, Louise Dunmall, for £300 the maximum allowed under the Workmen's Compensation Act. Judgement was given in favour of Louise Dunmall for £234 with costs. Leave was given to appeal, but after negotiations, Louise Dunmall accepted the sum of £200. Ellen was unable to attend court in person for by this time she was very frail. She died at Ravenswood on 17 May 1911 aged 89, and was buried alongside "dearest Emily".

Two months later the Coronation celebrations began for King George V. There were special church services, cricket matches, and pictures of the new King and Queen were unveiled in the village school by the

West Wickham Coronation Sports 1911

48

Lord of the Manor, Sir Henry Lennard, (Sir John Lennard died in 1900) followed by games and a tea for the children. There was a dance at Wickham Court attended by over 350 people. Coronation gifts were given to the old people and young mothers. The ladies were given a teapot, 1lb. tea and a Coronation plate. The gentlemen received tobacco and a Coronation plate. A new king was on the throne. The Sherrards took up residence at Ravenswood.

4. *The Sherrards of Ravenswood*

Ellen Hall left Ravenswood and its estate (excepting The Croft) to sister Louisa's son, Charles William Sherrard, now a retired Colonel in the Royal Engineers, and his sons, James, a Captain in the same regiment, and Owen. The Croft was bequeathed to a third son, Laurence, also a Captain in the Royal Engineers. Laurence was badly wounded in the fighting at Krohnstadt in South Africa in 1900.

Charles Sherrard, born on Christmas Day 1848, was educated at Rugby from whence he took a commission in 1870. He was an all-round athlete and played rugby for Blackheath, and was in the England side against Scotland in the Calcutta Cup in 1871. Charles was a first-class cricketer and played for Kent and Hampshire as well as being a member of the MCC and I. Zingari. During his army career Charles Sherrard was an Instructor of Fortifications at Woolwich and later went through the Zulu War in which he and his men suffered severe privations. He then went on to Jamaica where he married Clara. After that he was stationed in Malta where he was responsible for the building of fortifications. Charles Sherrard retired in 1901 and lived in Beckenham before inheriting Ravenswood.

West Wickham Rifle Club soon recruited the Colonel as its President who was emboldened enough to complain to the Bromley Rural District Council of the dirty and untidy condition of the road outside Ravenswood, at its worst on Mondays. (Presumably because of litter left by Sunday day-trippers.)

Charles Sherrard not only inherited Ravenswood and its untidy road, but also the troublesome public footpath over Ravenswood land. The West Wickham Parish Council wrote to Charles in January 1916 calling his attention to the unsatisfactory state of the path which, because its edges were lower than the adjacent meadow, was under water in wet weather. Charles disputed his liability in the matter, but after an interview with Sir Henry Lennard, Chairman of the Rural District Council, he agreed to foot the bill for the necessary repairs.

The Great War cast its shadow over the inhabitants of West Wickham. Charles' daughter Marjorie joined the West Wickham Voluntary Aid Detachment of the British Red Cross Society as a VAD, and as such, put in 1,343 hours of service at Warren House Red Cross Hospital. Charles himself served as a military representative at a London Military Service Tribunal.

Clara Maude Sherrard died in November 1919 and was buried in St. John's churchyard. At the time it seemed that West Wickham would remain a sleepy little village, but change was on the way. In 1922 Manor House, at the west end of the High Street, was sold as was the Monks Orchard estate on the Kent and Surrey borders. It had been Ellen Hall's wish (no more than that) that neither her nephew nor either of his sons "should sell the said property . . . for building purposes", but on 26 July 1922 Charles Sherrard gave notice to the Trustees that he intended selling Ravenswood and its adjoining land. At the ensuing auction John Howard from Bromley bought Lots 1,3,4 and 8 (see Map IV) — comprising Ravenswood and 17 acres of land; a four-roomed gardener's cottage; four cottages and Ivy Lodge in Station Road; and 1 & 2 Croft Cottages in the High Street. John Howard paid £6,000 for his purchases.

Charles Sherrard then moved to 57 Wickham Road, Beckenham where he died in 1938 aged 89, and was buried in Sidlow Bridge Cemetery, Reigate. James Sherrard, Charles' son, was commissioned into the Indian Army, retiring with the rank of Lieutenant Colonel. James died two years after being appointed CBE in 1924 for services rendered in the field in connection with military operations in Wazirastan during 1922 and 1923. Owen went on to become an author of several notable works, including *The Life of Chatham*. He also wrote *Two Victorian Girls,* using the diaries of his great-aunts Emily and Ellen Hall, but died in 1962, four years before the book was published. Laurence Sherrard died at Brighton in 1936.

Ravenswood and its lands sold in 1922

Lot 1: The house — Ravenswood — together with its outbuildings, a range of buildings, pleasure garden and grounds together with a 4-roomed gardener's cottage — an area of 17a 3r 18p.

Lot 2: Ten acres of meadow land in a triangle formed by Beckenham Road, and what are now Ravenswood Crescent and Blake Recreation Ground.

Lot 3: Four cottages at Wickham Green and a cottage with a shop and an adjoining plot of land.

Lot 4: Two cottages — Ivy Cottage and Ivy Lodge in Station Road on the site of the West Wickham Swimming Pools.

Lot 5: White Gate Farm with meadow land, a smallholding of five acres running up from Station Road from the West Wickham Swimming Pools site, with a small frontage to Hawes Lane.

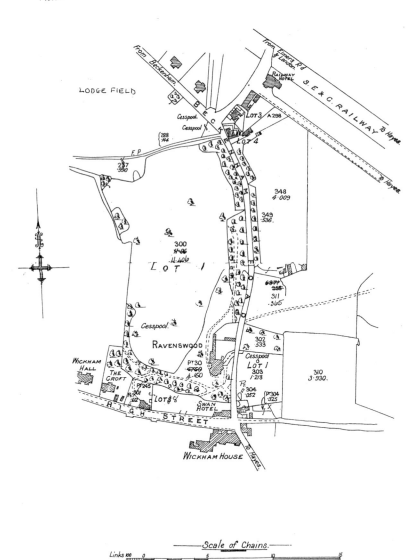

RAVENSWOOD ESTATE

1922

IV — Lots 1, 3, 4 and 8 purchased by John Howard

(Sold prior to the auction) It was later converted to a Tea and Store Room by Mrs. Mary Coote.

Lot 6: Six acres of meadow land just off the High Street fronting what is now Glebe Way, between the library and the former Fire Station.

Lot 7: Yew Tree Cottage and The Forge opposite The Swan public house in Station Road. Yew Tree Cottage was sold prior to the auction. It was demolished in 1939. The Forge was bought by its tenants, Tombling & Nottle.

Lot 8: 1 & 2 Croft Cottage in the High Street almost opposite what is now The Grove.

Lot 9: Three acres of meadow land just off the High Street and now developed as Barwood Avenue. (Sold prior to auction)

Ravenswood in 1922 (as described in the Sale Particulars)

"The Property comprises a most Substantially Brick Built Detached Family Residence standing in Beautiful Pleasure Grounds approached by Carriage Sweep with two Gateway Entrances leading up the Principal Entrance.

ON THE GROUND FLOOR

A Fine Lofty Oak Panelled Entrance Hall about 30ft.6in. long by 12ft.6in. wide, with polished oak parquet floor, open fireplace, and old-fashioned dog grate; directly leading to

An Exceedingly Pretty Heated Conservatory or Winter Garden with shaped glass dome roof (measuring about 27ft.6in. by 20ft.6in.), tessellated and decorated tiled floor, four brick-edged Fernery Beds and centre ornamental ditto, all planted with choice Palms, Grasses and various Ferns.

Charming Boudoir about 25ft.6in. by 14ft., fitted stove and marble mantelpiece, moulded frieze border to ceiling, Side Door to Garden; also pair large Double doors which can, for entertaining purposes, be opened into an

Elegant Drawing Room, about 33ft. by 18ft., fitted stove and marble mantelpiece, with large bay window and French Casement Doors opening to Garden and Grounds.

Excellent and Well-Proportioned Dining Room, about 23ft.6in. by 17ft., fitted stove and marble mantelpiece.

53

Cottages at Wickham Green — note the Leather Bottle predecessor to The Railway Hotel

White Gate Farm/Ye Olde Dairy Farm

54

Tombling & Nottle

Yew Tree Cottage c1910   *Ida Bennee*

Cosy Library about 15ft.6in. by 15ft., fitted stove and painted mantelpiece; Side Door opening to Court Yard.

Capital Bath Room fitted with modern white enamelled bath, lavatory basin (hot and cold supplies); Store Cupboard. Separate W.C.

The Domestic Offices are on the same level, well shut off and very complete. They include:–

Back Hall with radiator
Secondary Staircase
Still Room, about 16ft. by 12ft.6in., fitted heated Linen Cupboards, Deep Sink (hot and cold supplies)
Maids' Sitting Room, about 10ft.6in. by 10ft., with fireplace Butler's Pantry, fitted sink (Hot and cold), Dresser and Store Cupboards.
Large and Lofty Kitchen, about 19ft.6in. by 16ft.6in., fitted with modern Kitchener, 10ft. Dresser and Store Cupboards
Scullery, with Sink (hot and cold supplies), Return Dresser
Larder
Extra Store Room, with entrance from Court Yard
Servants' W.C.
Coal Store and Wine Cellars

ON THE FIRST FLOOR

Approached by the easy and well-lighted Fine Oak Panelled Staircase with Gallery Landings are the Four Principal Bedchambers measuring respectively about 21ft.6in. by 18ft., 13ft. by 11ft.6in., 17ft.6in. by 17ft., and 17ft. by 15ft., all fitted with fireplaces.

Dressing Room about 16ft. by 15ft.

Ante Room about 16ft. by 15ft.

Charming Room (with Balcony overlooking the Grounds), about 40ft. by 19ft., fitted Register Stove, tiled sides, marble jambs, and handsome three-tier oak mantelpiece. Heating Radiator in Enclosure. Fine Moulded Panel Ceiling.

Back Landing with Housemaid's Sink.
Separate W.C.
Secondary Staircase.

ON THE SECOND FLOOR

Five Well-Proportioned Bedrooms measuring respectively about 13ft. by 12ft., 16ft. by 12ft., 19ft. by 9ft., 21ft. by 12ft., and 13ft. by 12ft. Two fitted with fireplaces

Box Room
Landing and Passage

THE OUTBUILDINGS have a separate double gateway entrance and comprise:–

Capital Brick-Built Detached Stabling and Garage with five Loose Boxes.

Large Garage, about 23ft. by 20ft.6in. with outside cement washdown, covered by glass roof.

Saddle Room and Four Rooms over for man

also

RANGE OF BUILDINGS   including

Large Fruit Store   Shed with small Shed adjoining.
Two Bee-Houses.   Wood Sheds.   Granary.
Boot House.   Stoke Hole.   W.C.

Paved Court Yard with Two Small Grass Lawns and gravelled walks.

The Beautiful Pleasure Garden and Grounds are a feature of the Property. They are nicely timbered and contain a choice collection of specimen Trees and Shrubs, the whole being exceptionally well laid out in the most splendid condition, including a Fine Tennis Lawn, Croquet Lawn, Flower Borders, Parterres, Winding Gravel Walks and Paths through Woodlands. Fine old Acacia, Chestnut, Elm and Lime Trees, with Park-like Meadow. Excellent Walled Kitchen Garden and Orchard containing pretty Pergola, numerous trained Fruit Trees in full bearing, Asparagus and Rhubarb Beds etc.

Lean-to Greenhouse about 32ft. by 10ft., Heated Vinery, 22ft. by 13ft.6in. Range of Five Brick-built Forcing Pits with lights. Tool Store and Potting Shed. Also Flower Garden with Box Borders and Yew Hedges.

Together with Four-Roomed Gardener's Cottage, the whole embracing an area of 17a 3r 18p."

5. *Ravenswood Hotel*

John Howard, having successfully bid for Ravenswood at auction, proceeded to transform the house into a hotel, adding more bathrooms in the process. Emily Hall's croquet lawn became a feature of the hotel's facilities which also included two tennis courts, and bowling and putting greens.

John Howard also owned Runswick House in the High Street. The building, bearing the date '1865', had in its time housed a butcher's shop with a slaughter-house at the rear, and later a baker's shop. John Howard renamed the building Ravenswood Annexe, and a cafe was opened on the premises. An application for a licence to sell wine and spirits was refused.

Ravenswood as a hotel was not a success and so both Ravenswood Hotel and Ravenswood Annexe were sold. The hotel was sold to Harold

Runswick House — to right of tree

Dowler and John Turrell who resold it to Kent & Surrey Estates Ltd. In 1926 this company sold Ravenswood Hotel and adjoining lands to George Spencer, a builder from Norbury. Barclays Bank acquired Ravenswood Annexe and in 1928 opened a branch of the bank, sub to its Shirley branch, upgrading it to full branch status two years later. Barclays Bank has, over the years, substantially altered the premises, both externally and internally, but the former Runswick House is still an imposing building worthy of its inclusion on Bromley Borough's 'Local List' of buildings, and so while not statutorily protected, it will be left undisturbed as far as possible.

6. *The Spencers of Ravenswood*

Once more Ravenswood became a family home. George Spencer and his wife Selina had three sons, George, Charles and Herbert, and a daughter Eva, but even they found Ravenswood too large for their use. The problem was solved by converting Ravenswood into two units, renaming the northern half Hamilton House, which eventually became the property of M. A. Ray & Sons Ltd., builders' merchants. George Spencer and his family continued to live in their half of Ravenswood. In 1928 Hamilton House was leased to William Tudor-Davies who there established Wickham College with himself as headmaster. More of Wickham College later.

George Spencer snr., a builder, as well as being a devoted family man, was an accomplished artist, gardener and a keen cine-cameraman, recording events in and around Wickham. Amateur dramatics featured high in domestic entertainment and various scenarios were enacted in and around Ravenswood and captured on film, to be shown many years later to appreciative audiences by George's grandsons. One film was shot inside the then Collett's chemists, of 13 High Street.

There was a legend that a French ambassador had been killed in a duel with the Duke of Hamilton at Ravenswood and that he was buried under the huge urn in the grounds. Another legend had it that he was buried under the cobble-stones in the courtyard. The Spencer family decided to investigate the urn but the only bones found under it were thought to be those of a dog. A Croydon stonemason bought the urn and in ensuing years it was used for floral displays at exhibitions. George Spencer snr., in an interview with the compilers of the *Ravenswood Women's Institute Scrapbook* (1956), said that had also removed a "three-holer outside privy" from the grounds.

George Spencer jnr. married Iris May Bush in 1927 and they lived in a house called The Pantiles, built for them by George Spencer snr. on the Wickham House Estate. The pantiles used in the new house were taken from the outbuildings of Wickham House (owned by George Spencer snr.) as were the stable doors which were used to make the garage. The Pantiles was originally designed to front Woodland Way but with an 800-year-old oak tree in the proposed front garden, George

Spencer chose to retain the tree and build the house to back on to Woodland Way, and to become part of Park Avenue. However, the lay-out for the new roads on the Wickham House Estate was changed and Park Avenue, from being a much grander road, was reduced in area and, in the process, The Pantiles became 2 Southcroft Avenue.

Charles Spencer married Eveline (Bessie) Killick, daughter of Joseph of the building firm of J. & R. Killick, in 1931 and the wedding reception was held, as was brother George's, at Ravenswood. Charles and Bessie set up home in another Spencer house — Tudor House — in Woodland Way.

Wedding group at Ravenswood 12 September 1931

L – R

Back row: George Killick; Miss Louise Killick; George Spencer Jnr.; Mrs. Iris Spencer; Herbert Spencer

Middle row: James Killick; Harry Ellson; Mrs. Ethel Ellson; Mrs. Edith Killick; Harold Stockbridge (Best man); Mrs. Selina Spencer; George Spencer Snr.; Mrs. Eva Foad; George Foad

Front row: Miss Joan Killick; Miss Grace Killick; Alan Ellson;. Charles Spencer (Bridegroom); Mrs. Eveline Spencer (Bride); Miss Eva Spencer; Miss Joy Ellson *David Spencer*

In 1932 George Spencer's half of Ravenswood was demolished to make way for a cinema. The stables and the old bake-house were sold to M. A. Ray & Sons Ltd., and part of the garden was sold as a site for a new Crown Post Office, for by this time Wickham's population had soared to 6,229 and the small village Post Office in the High Street was unable to cope.

George Spencer snr. then moved to one of two houses he had built in the grounds of Ravenswood. (The other house was for his gardener, Ernest Bartholomew who tended the gardens of both Wickham College and Ravenswood). Ravenscroft was the name given to the Spencer home with its woodwork, both external and internal, being found from old ships' timbers. The Spencer Family Bible proudly records the use of Ravenscroft for robing purposes and hospitality by various dignitaries including Cosmo Lang, then Archbishop of Canterbury, when the foundation stone of St. Francis' church was laid, and again when the church was consecrated in 1936.

Another Spencer left the nest in 1935 when Eva, a talented amateur actress, married John Crawshaw in the parish church. Herbert joined the Army on the outbreak of war in 1939.

George Spencer built houses of quality in West Wickham and Hayes (having also acquired Pickhurst Manor and other land in Hayes) and even today a 'Spencer' house is marketable by name alone. Builders in

Ravenscroft   *Herbert Spencer*

Wickham were not always popular with the villagers but George Spencer, while developing large areas of land, gained great respect for his sympathetic approach. He even gained the support of Mrs. Catherine Bellringer, a formidable parish councillor who, at a public inquiry in April 1932 on the building line in Station Road, declared that "Mr. Spencer had done more for the development of West Wickham than the rest of the builders. He had done all he could to retain the beauties of the place."

George Spencer died at Ravenscroft in 1963, and his wife two years later, both spared the knowledge that Ravenscroft would be subject to a compulsory purchase order in 1966 (as was the gardener's house) to make way for a public car park.

7. *The Plaza Cinema*

George Spencer's half of Ravenswood had been demolished in October 1932 to make way for a cinema. A Plaza Cinema, promoted by Modern Cinemas Ltd., and designed by J. Stanley Beard & Clare, was duly opened on 4 September 1933 with its own Plaza Orchestra. Mrs. Beam's 'Breezy Babes' performed; a tenor, Robert Hargreaves, sang. There was a fanfare, a speech and then the first films were screened — Mickey Mouse in 'Mickey's Nightmare', 'So this is Africa', and 'Our Betters' starring Constance Bennett.

Demolition of part of Ravenswood 1932

Post Office & Odeon Cinema 1950   *Bromley Central Library*

Station Road showing Gaumont Cinema

Plaza Cinema

In 1939, just before the Second World War, the Plaza was acquired by the Odeon circuit and renamed the Odeon. During the War the cinema was also used by the Home Guard for recruiting purposes. The building was damaged on 7 October 1940 when a bomb fell in Ravenswood Avenue, hurling heavy masses of concrete incredible distances. One large piece crashed through the roof of the cinema, slightly injuring two soldiers. The patrons were prepared to sit it out but the performance had to be discontinued because light was showing through a hole in the roof.

The Odeon Cinema Club (a junior Saturday Club) established before the War, continued to flourish after the cinema became a 'Gaumont' in 1951.

The popularity of cinema-going declining with the advent of television, coupled with a high entertainment tax, were the reasons given by the cinema's then owners, the J. Arthur Rank Organisation, for closing the Plaza/Odeon/Gaumont at West Wickham in January 1957. Ironically enough, the cinema, with a seating capacity of 896, had a full house for the last performance. 'Whisky' the cat, who had migrated to the cinema from The Swan some years before, found a new home with a member of the staff.

The West Wickham Community Council did consider the possibility of purchasing the cinema, on sale for £20,000, and adapting it as a community centre but abandoned the scheme which would have cost in the region of £45,000. The cinema was eventually demolished and a supermarket — Fine Fare — was opened on the site in 1962, itself to be replaced by a branch of Boots the Chemists in 1971.

Demolition of cinema 1961   *Harry Walden*

8. *Wickham College*

Wickham College opened in the northern half of Ravenswood in 1928 with William Tudor-Davies as its headmaster. A reporter from the *Beckenham Journal* visited the school soon after it opened — "High up upon the North Wall can be seen the original leaded windows . . . and in places the old lead water spouts are fitted. The old courtyard with the stable and outhouses, and the house surrounding it on three sides, is still discernible and the cobble-stones peep out amongst the grass and the later dated flagstones. In the courtyard stands the original pump complete with leaden spout. The room in which the students take their lessons was originally the kitchen. It is a curious apartment with narrow oak beams and white plaster in between. The huge fireplace, denuded of its original grate, is also believed to be Tudor."

Courtyard — north view   *Bromley Central Library*

Dining-room at Wickham College   *Bromley Central Library*

The entrance to the hall was through the courtyard. The former dining-room was used for art lessons, including pewter work. The tutor for the artistic part of the syllabus was Mrs. Tudor-Davies who designed and made a crucifix for the first St. Francis church in the High Street. Other staff included Miss Olive James (French), Miss Gwendoline Shaw (Mathematics), Mr. Beynon (English), and the two daughters of William Tudor-Davies — Elaine and Irene. On fine days lessons were given in the grounds of Wickham College. After Blake Recreation Ground was opened in 1932, games and athletics were held there. At other times use was made of McAndrew Park.

Wickham College, initially, had 34 boy pupils aged five to thirteen years, but it later became a co-educational school with a nursery class for the three to five-year-olds. Candidates were entered for examinations set by the College of Preceptors, Oxford and Cambridge Locals, London Matriculation and Public School entrance. The school colours were green and brown, the girls' summer dresses being made of shantung. The school badge was a Tudor rose.

William Tudor-Davies became involved in local affairs and took part in the organising of the West Wickham Fair and Flitch in 1933. This particular fair caused some consternation when a knife-thrower, performing his act, unexpectedly inflicted a wound on the arm of the lady acting as a human target! In 1937 William Tudor-Davies was succeeded as head of Wickham College by Miss Olive James.

Jean Pinnington was a pupil at Wickham College in the 30s. "We

Wickham College staff and pupils 1930 *Ivor Davies*

had some unusual instruction . . . Once we were taken to a field where sheep had rubbed off bits of their wool on the fence. We collected it . . . picked thistles and the straightest twig we could find. Back at school we made a clay cake, thrust the twig through it . . . we had a spindle each. We teazled the wool on the thistles and spun it . . . The Wickham College boys and the village schoolboys were terrific enemies and running fights ensued. The village boys tended to shriek 'W.C.' whenever they saw us. A tactless badge to have to wear."

Shelagh Akester (now Rogers), also a pupil in the 30s, was taught French at the age of seven. "The College was ahead of its time" in this respect. "Effort was appreciated and encouraged, and having done particularly well with spelling," Shelagh "was presented with a smart blue leather purse with a white leather lining, containing five shillings, at the annual prize-day."

War was declared on 3 September 1939 and all schools were closed. Wickham College re-opened within a few weeks after a shelter was constructed in the former wine cellar where "poor wretched Jane" had disgraced herself in 1867. Dariel Davies (now Raven), a pupil in the 40s, remembers the air raid shelter "constructed by making a new entrance to the cellar beneath my form room and installing benches and electric light. It was very cold and damp. In wartime winter the Tudor fireplace belched smoke into our panelled form room, but little heat. My fingertips used to turn white. To warm us up, we were taken outside to exercise on the flagstones every breaktime. There was no ceiling — you looked up to plaster and wooden beams under the pitched roof, and a small bell-cote." By this time Miss Olive James and Miss Kathleen Ford had become joint heads of the College.

Shelagh Bodle (now Hoblyn) remembers the legend that there was a secret passage to Wickham Court from the little door halfway up the stairs. Another "secret passage" began in the former wine cellar now converted into an air raid shelter.

Wickham College was one of several private schools in West Wickham before the War. The demand was there, for with a population explosion

71

Round door at Ravenswood   *Bromley Central Library*

— 1,301 in 1921; 6,229 in 1931; 10,080 in 1934; 20,000 approximately in 1939 — the local authority was having trouble in containing the situation. The War presented problems of a different nature. The combination of wartime restraints — evacuation, air raids and staff shortages — took its toll in both the private and public sectors. The building required constant repairs from blast damage, and that received in 1944 when a flying-bomb exploded nearby in Links Road, caused structural damage. The College closed sometime after 1943 (probably after the flying-bomb campaign began in June 1944). It was demolished in 1957 to make way for a petrol station and a car showroom for S. G. Smith (Motors) Ltd. which opened two years later, numbered 84-86 Station Road.

In 1961 J. Sainsbury Ltd., having bought the buildings and adjacent land at 76-82 Station Road owned by M. A. Ray & Sons Ltd., put in a successful planning application to develop the site with a self-service store. Sainsbury's eventually closed its existing shop in the High Street and opened a supermarket in Station Road in May 1964. The *Kentish Times* reported that "the ladies looked very smart in their Hardy Amies-designed overalls of pale blue nylon. Lord Sainsbury visited the store . . . and his eldest son, Mr. J. D. Sainsbury, was present when the doors were opened."

J. Sainsbury supermarket 1964   *J. Sainsbury plc*

And so the story of Ravenswood ends. There is now no visible evidence of the existence of Ravenswood the house, but the presence in the Station Road/Ravenswood Avenue area of a few protected 'Ravenswood' trees stirs memories of its former glory.

The Croft

The Croft

The Croft was an 18th century house on the northern side of the High Street, situated between what is now Ravenswood Avenue and Braemar Gardens. It dated from around 1743 and was built on the site, and in the place of, one formerly called Brooke House. It is possible, with the aid of the parish Poor-Rate and Church-Rate books to identify with some certainty the names of the early tenants:–

1763 – 1764 Mayhew Marrett
1765 – 1773 Captain Langton
1776   Fry
1777 – 1778 Mr. Dunlop
1779   Mr. Spottiswoode
1780 – 1784 Mr. Swaddle
1785   Samuel Beachcroft
1786 – 1809 John Scott
1812 – 1820 Charles Law
1822 – 1924 Mr. Butler
1827 – 1837 John Anderson
1838 – 1839 Mrs. Price (named on the 1838 Tithe Listings)

Little is known of these tenants excepting Samuel Beachcroft, a London merchant, who, although he lived at The Croft for only one year, was no stranger to West Wickham having leased Wickham Court, the manor house, from 1765 to 1775. He was also a director of the Bank of England and its governor from 1775 to 1777. When Samuel Beachcroft died in 1797 he was buried in St. John's churchyard, as was his wife Elizabeth who died seven years later. Both Samuel and Elizabeth Beachcroft have their hatchments hanging in the parish church.

Another early tenant, when Peter Burrell III owned the property was John Scott who served West Wickham as overseer of the poor on several occasions, and was a Freeman of the Watermen's Company of the Thames. He was able to use his status as a Freeman to claim exemption from having to supply the Militia with a horse and a man during the Napoleonic Wars when invasion threatened England. John Scott died in 1809.

Peter Burrell III, later created Lord Gwydir, died in 1820 and his estates were broken up and sold. The Croft was purchased at auction for £820 by two brothers, John and Fr[ancis?] Miller. The Croft then had a farm and outbuildings and stood in three acres of land.

From 1841 the census returns and other sources are much more helpful and The Croft becomes more than just a property owned by the Miller brothers. The Revd. Samuel Doria, described in the 1841 census as a 30-year-old mathematician, used The Croft as a small boarding school whose six pupils' ages ranged from eight to seventeen years. The good reverend's wife Susan had already presented her husband with three sons and a daughter and so needed the assistance of three servants and a governess to run this rather youthful household. Susan Doria bore three more children while at West Wickham, the last of whom, Susan, lived for less than a week. The Revd. Samuel Doria occasionally preached in the parish church and, in so doing, earned Emily Hall's approval on at least one occasion. She wrote of him in her diary in April 1844 — "Mr. Doria is actually of the Spinetta family — he does not show his breeding. Gave us a very good sermon today." One can imagine the serried ranks of the Doria household listening (or not listening) on that particular Sunday.

The Croft was added to sometime during this period. Again Emily Hall was the reporter — "Mr. Doria the schoolmaster had 14 boys in that house *before* it was enlarged."

The Dorias lived at The Croft until at least 1846. Then in 1853 Dr. Samuel Solly, who owned a house in London's Savile Row, became the tenant at The Croft. Dr. Solly was a surgeon and Lecturer in Surgery at St. Thomas' Hospital and was one of the last of the surgeons to a London hospital who succeeded to his post by virtue of having paid a large apprenticeship fee. He was also an artist and his water-colours were exhibited more than once at the Royal Academy. Dr. Solly died in 1871 and was buried at Chislehurst. After his death a marble bust was presented to St. Thomas' Hospital. Following Dr. Solly at The Croft were "Mrs. Smith" (1855) and "Dale Esq." (1858).

Henry and Constance Pott took up their abode at The Croft in 1859 after which Mrs. Pott produced, at intervals, Henry, Frances, Constance, Jessie, Arthur and Annie. It was during the Pott's tenure of The Croft that its ownership changed hands once more when Emily and Ellen Hall paid £1,600 for the house and yard which, in the late 18th century, had been the village cock-pit. Emily was amused enough to write of the vendors that the "Miller at Horley is even a greater miser than his brother at Norwood. They are described in their deeds of purchase as 'ironmongers' — in their deeds of sale, as 'gentlemen'. Such is the effect from having retired from business."

The increasing size of the Pott household evidently produced problems, for Henry Pott offered to buy The Croft so that he could enlarge it. The offer was rejected by Emily and Ellen who neither wished to sell nor to enlarge The Croft, so very reluctantly the Pott family left West Wickham in 1866.

Some essential repairs to The Croft were put in hand in 1867 and it was while the work was in progress and being inspected by Emily Hall that Captain Alfred Torrens, of the 66th Regiment, and his fiancée, Miss Ann Scott, called to view the house. "In the most outspoken way he told Em his intention and wishes and income — 'The fact is I am going to marry a daughter of Sir Claude Scott [of Sundridge Park] and I am hoping to get the adjutancy of the Croydon Volunteers and I must have a house with stables within reach of Croydon — my income will be about £1,200 a year . . .'" A week later Captain Torrens and his lady agreed terms with Emily and Ellen. The sisters were soon to regret their choice of tenants. Even before the wedding took place, the future Mrs. Torrens complained (possible with some justification) that the yard had not been cleared, the floors were dirty and that the fruit in the garden had been pilfered. Soon after the newly-weds moved in, Mrs. Torrens had to deal with a burst cistern and so demanded a replacement from Emily. A "very large cesspool" was also required "or diphtheria may be the consequence". The Torrens left for Baston Manor in Hayes in 1873.

William Courthope, a Civil Servant at the Privy Council office, his wife Mary and one-year-old Katharine came to live at The Croft in 1875. Ellen Hall approved of the new tenants who "seem to be pleasant cultivated people. She decidedly pretty and very ladylike." The family soon grew with the addition of three sons, John (1876), Edward (1880) and Richard (1882). On the night of the 1881 census it was recorded that William, Mary and their (then) three children were at home together with Mary's own personal maid, Louisa Yerby; the nurse, Mary Blake; the parlour maid, Fanny Akers; and Sarah Coventry, the nursery-maid. Also, visiting were William's sister Anna and her own personal maid, Swiss-born Verena Ralisberger. The Courthopes lived at The Croft very happily until 1887 when they left for pastures new.

The following year, after protracted negotiations, a church architect, John Sedding, took a 21-year lease of The Croft — protracted because he required a great many improvements and alterations to the property, to which Emily was reluctant to agree, despite the fact that John Sedding was prepared to make certain improvements himself. In fact John Sedding was so delighted with The Croft that he enquired if it were for sale.

The required alterations proceeded, although not without some difficulties, for George Dumbrell, a local bricklayer employed at The Croft, told Emily Hall that "Mr. Sedding seems not to know his own mind — keeps on altering." This was in July 1888. Two months later Emily wrote in her diary, "Had a long talk with Dumbrell . . . He talked of the trouble he had over The Croft work — Mr. Sedding being an artist and not practical . . . and has continually altered it after it was done!" However, all was eventually finished to John Sedding's satisfaction and he and his young family moved from their London home in Charlotte Street. The family in 1888 consisted of John, his wife Rose (a daughter of Canon Tinling of Gloucester), and three children — Dorothy, George and Edward. Emily and Ellen Hall were invited to visit The Croft. Ellen recorded the visit — "The drawing-room is wonderfully pretty. He has removed the folding doors and thrown out a bow into the garden, which fills up the whole of that side — he has decorated it charmingly. The dining-room he has enlarged and panelled, putting plates in each square at the top of the dado . . ."

John Sedding

John Sedding, elected an F.R.I.B.A. in 1874, was an important figure in the Arts & Crafts Movement and primarily a church architect. He was a member of the Art Worker's Guild established in 1884, and became its second Master. By 1880 John Sedding had an office in Oxford Street in London where he took on as assistants, Henry Wilson and John Paul Cooper who both became silversmiths and jewellers, and Ernest Gimson, later to become a furniture designer. A few years later Alfred Powell joined the firm. He was to decorate pottery for Wedgewood.

John and Rose Sedding soon became members of the congregation of West Wickham's parish church where the architect offered his services and financial help in re-designing the interior of the church. The subsequent faculty allowed for the removal of existing seats, floors, organ and heating apparatus; the removal and re-fixing of the font and pulpit; the erection of new oak seating; the building of an organ chamber opening into the chancel; the formation of a vestry in the tower porch; and the opening out of the old vestry to receive the font. John Sedding, no mean organist himself, also designed the organ front with linenfold and twisted carvings to the panel and frame, thus complementing the medieval rood screen embellishments. He had a deep love of flowers and used flowers and leaves constantly to decorate his work — much in evidence in St. John's chancel pews.

The alterations to the seating involved the loss of private pews, a source of anguish to several of the congregation, especially to Emily and Ellen Hall, John Sedding's landlords!

In 1890 John Sedding designed a house in West Wickham called Springfield. Emily Hall wrote in her diary that "Mrs. Thomasett is building a huge house opposite that German tradesman [Gustav Mellin of Wickham Hall] . . . Mr. Sedding is the architect — not *my* taste — but rather good." This "rather good house" has survived the incursions of the 20th century into West Wickham and is currently a Dr. Barnado's non-residential school known as Knotley School, in Springfield Gardens.

Tragedy struck the Sedding family in 1891 when John Sedding, while engaged on restoration work at Winsford Vicarage in Somerset, contracted pleurisy. John sent for his wife Rose who arrived with a five-month-old baby in her arms, having despatched the three eldest children to her father. Also to help care for the patient came a trained nurse and a brother-in-law, Dr. Browne, a physician at St. Bartholomew's Hospital. After an illness lasting less than a week. John Sedding died on 7 April at the relatively early age of 52. Two days before he died John Sedding told the Revd. E. F. Russell he had "to thank God for the happiest of homes and the sweetest of wives".

At the wish of Rose Sedding, a grave was prepared at West Wickham.

Springfield and Springfield Lodge

The Solemn Requeim, by her wish also, was to be held at the church where John Sedding had served both as sidesman and churchwarden, St. Alban's the Martyr in Holborn. Rose Sedding began her journey home to attend the funeral but she had covered only ten miles before she too was struck down with pleurisy. She died at Dulverton eight days after her husband's demise. Among Rose Sedding's papers were found, written in her own hand, the following lines of a 17th century poet:

> "Tis fit one flesh should have
> One tomb, one epitaph, one grave,
> And as they that lived and loved either
> Should dye, and lye, and sleep together"

John and Rose Sedding "lye and sleep together" in St. John's churchyard where their tombstone is aptly decorated with trailing flowers and leaves. Nearby is the grave of their son George who died of wounds received as a soldier fighting in France in the First World War.

Between 1880 and his death in 1891 John Sedding built, among other works:–

> All Saints Vicarage, Plymouth
> Church of the Holy Redeemer, Clerkenwell

82

St. Augustine's, Highgate
St. Edward's Netley
All Saints, Falmouth
St. Dyfrig's, Cardiff
Salcombe Church, Devon
The Children's Hospital Frindsbury
St. Peter's, Ealing (with Henry Wilson)
Holy Trinity Church, Sloane Street,
(unfinished)

Emily and Ellen Hall were greatly distressed by the tragedy — "When he took The Croft on a 21-year-lease, who could have imagined that his time was so shortly to cease! and that *we* should be his survivors! He seemed hardly to have entered on the enjoyment of the place he had arranged with so much taste . . . It is a tragedy . . . with two such young and vigorous people."

A K. C., James Rolt, expressed interest in leasing The Croft and enquired if he might sub-let the stables. Emily Hall was agreeable to this providing that they were not let to Dr. William Blake, the village doctor. Apparently Dr. Blake had testified for Sophia Neville, who had successfully sued the Halls for injuries received in a fall when using the stile in Lodge Field on the Ravenswood estate. In the event The Croft was let to Mrs. Snow, James Rolt's mother-in-law, who was soon joined by her two young married daughters and their respective spouses — Katherine, and Arthur Gripper, a corn merchant, and Grace, James' wife. Babies soon made their appearances — John Rolt in 1890; Philip Rolt and Mary Gripper in 1892; and Patience Gripper in 1895. The Grippers moved out of The Croft soon after Patience's birth and set up home in Laurel Cottage at the western end of the High Street, close to The White Hart (and where part of Squire's Timber Yard is now). Arthur Gripper was one of the six children of Edward Gripper of Oak Lodge, five of whom set up their own establishments in West Wickham. As Ellen Hall wrote in her diary in 1898, "the village is well and truly 'Grippered'"

The Rolts continued the lease of The Croft. Ellen liked Mrs. Grace Rolt, noting that "she is pleasant and like a lady and is among the very few in this exalted village who can lay claim to so much. Except Mrs. McAndrew, all the others are different shades of Grippers." Both the Rolts and the various members of the Gripper clan were prominent in the social life of the village, especially in amateur theatricals and concerts staged in the Lecture Hall (now the Pop-in-Parlour) in Sussex Road.

When war came in 1914 both the Rolt boys joined the Army. Philip, a tea planter in Ceylon, enlisted in the Ceylon Contingent of the Indian

The Croft prior to demolition

Croft Parade 1994   *Joyce Walker*

Army and was gazetted a Lieutenant in the 27th Punjab Regiment and saw service in Egypt, France and Mesopotamia. He was Mentioned in Despatches in 1916. John, an engineer, joined the Army Service Corps and served in France, and was also Mentioned in Despatches. Their cousins, Patience and Mary Gripper, became Red Cross VADs and nursed at the local Red Cross Hospital at Warren House, where their mother, Commandant of the local Voluntary Aid Detachment, was in charge.

James Rolt was a popular figure in West Wickham. Amongst the offices he held was that of President of the West Wickham Bowling Club, having succeeded the Revd. Bertie Roberts in that post. James Rolt left West Wickham in 1927.

Robert Wilkinson followed as a very short-term tenant, for The Croft, which in 1911, had been bequeathed by Ellen Hall to her great-nephew, Laurence Sherrard, was sold for re-development and by 1933 The Croft Parade of shops had come into being.

Manor House

Manor House

Manor House (not be confused with *the* manor house, Wickham Court, in Layhams Road, the home of the Lord of the Manor), stood at the western end of the High Street, facing south and opposite what is now a Safeways supermarket. As far as is known Manor House was built around the turn of the 19th century, possibly earlier. In 1820 Judge Burton Morice owned the house. When he died in 1825 and was buried in the parish church of St. John the Baptist, Manor House passed to his brother John who lived there for nearly twenty years until his death in 1844. At the ensuing auction the house was sold for £4,000 to William Dallas. The Sale Particulars describe the property thus:–

"The House

Faces towards the South standing on a richly planted lawn approached from the Principal Entrance by a Covered Way which communicates with a handsome paved Verandah extending along the entire Front and round the Bow of the Drawing Room on the West, and contains,

On the TWO UPPER STORIES six servants and Secondary Bed Rooms with Closets; two large principal Bed Rooms with Dressing Room to each; two other best Bed Rooms; Water Closet; front and back Staircases.

Ground Floor: A Portland stone paved corridor and Vestibule; handsomely finished Bow Drawing Room 22′ x 18′6″, with French casement windows opening to the Lawn, communicating by folding doors with a Library 16′ x 14′; a lofty Dining-room with stuccoed walls 21′ x 17′, finished in good taste; Footman's Pantry; Housekeeper's Room; and W.C.

The OFFICES: A good kitchen with Dressers and Cupboards; Scullery and Wash-house, in which are a Brick Oven and two pumps of hard and soft water; Servants' Hall; Dairy and Cool Larder and exceedingly good open and lock-up cellars for Wine and general purposes.

IN THE COURT or STABLE YARD

Which lies well connected with the House is a capital well-finished four-stall Stable, with Man's Room and Loft over, a two-stall stable, Saddle Room, two Coach Houses, Laundry; and other conveniences.

SMALL FARM YARD

With a range of open and close Shedding; Cow House; Calf Pens; excellent Piggeries; Stowage for Hay and Straw.

A LARGE PRODUCTIVE GARDEN

Nearly Walled-in, of ³/₄ of an Acre, abundantly supplied with Standard and Wall Fruit Trees, of a good description, in which are both:

GREEN AND HOT HOUSES, WELL-STOCKED WITH CHOICE GRAPEVINES

The Grounds about the House are admirably disposed in Lawn, Flower Beds, Shrubbery and Pleasure Ground, to the extent of about an Acre;

Burton (or John) Morice

the residue being divided into convenient Paddocks, ornamented with fine Timber; and containing with the Cottages, herein after described about

13a 3r 0p

The three cottages and gardens, which join the High Road near the Stable Yard, are let to Messrs Johnson, Relf and Muggridge."

William and Louise Dallas and their family became part of Wickham's tightly-knit society and so appear in passing in the Hall diaries, even after the Dallas's had left Manor House in 1848/9. Where they went is not known but they do seem to have run into financial difficulties for Ellen wrote in January 1858 that "The Dallas' have just escaped bankruptcy — but have lost almost everything in the world." William Dallas has a commemorative wall tablet in St. John's church where he had been a churchwarden, recording the fact that he died at Hampstead in 1859 aged 65, and that he was buried in Brompton Cemetery.

Manor House 1845   *Bromley Central Library*

Six years later following a George Chilton, came 44-year-old Edward Vansittart Neale, wife Frances, and their five children, to make their mark on West Wickham. Edward Vansittart Neale was keenly interested in social reform and became a Christian Socialist and founder of the

91

Co-operative League, providing the inspiration and finance for various co-operative schemes, including the Co-operative Wholesale Society. However these schemes ran into difficulties, Edward Vansittart Neale losing £40,000 in the process. When he came to Manor House his income had dropped to around £1,500 a year. Nevertheless Henrietta, one of the daughters of the house, made a successful match when she married Henry Dickenson, son of William Dickenson, a wealthy merchant who lived nearby at Wickham Hall. The Vansittart Neales left West Wickham in 1868 for Shirley Cottage in Wickham Road, Shirley.

Much to Emily and Ellen's dismay Henry Brett, formerly of Beckenham, followed the Vansittart Neales at Manor House. "He is a Distiller and a very vulgar-looking man . . . who distils Brandy and placards the fact at Railway Stations and in advertisements in books . . ." Mrs. Harriet Brett was rated "rather better and is a pretty young woman." By 1875 there were eleven little Bretts living in Manor House as well as ten servants. The Bretts left West Wickham in 1880.

The Blaker family then moved in. Dr. Walter Blaker M.R.C.S. was only 31 years of age at the time but, according to Emily Hall, had "given up his work except as a charity here in the village and also at a dispensary in London." Emma Blaker, a year younger than her husband, was the mother of their three daughters, all born in Robertsbridge in Sussex. The household was completed by a governess and six servants.

A 51-year-old widow, Henrietta Thomasett, came to Manor House in 1886 but perhaps she was not entirely satisfied with the house for in 1890 she bought, from Sir John Lennard, a plot of land on the south side of the High Street. John Sedding, an architect who lived at The Croft, also in the High Street, was commissioned to design a house to be built on the land. It was named Springfield and Henrietta was able to move in in 1891.

Perhaps's Henrietta's decision to build a new house was influenced by the proximity of Manor House to the newly-built cottages on the former Pig Park, now Kent, Surrey, Sussex and North Roads. Emily Hall felt sorry for Henrietta Thomasett — "Pig Park covered with cottages of a wretched description without gardens or drains! filled with inhabitants, among whom children quite abound. The district is becoming a nuisance to the gentry, poor Mrs. Thomasett suffering much from it in hot weather."

The 1891 census listed some of the Thomasett family:– Claude aged 33; Victor a 23-year-old solicitor; Marguerite aged 21; and Bernard aged 18. Also in Manor House on the night of the Census were Ada Gripper, Henrietta's other daughter, together with her husband Harold Gripper, a son of Edward Gripper of Oak Lodge; and their one-year-old son Edward. Looking after their needs were a butler, a cook, a housemaid, a parlour maid and a kitchen maid. Henrietta Thomasett's household diminished when Victor married and set up house in Beckenham where his wife Eulalie gave birth to Gurden Theodore in 1894. Sadly Gurden Thomasett will be remembered for evermore for he is named on West Wickham's War Memorial as a casualty of the Battle of Loos in 1915, when he was serving as a Lieutenant in the 20th London Regiment.

The Thomasett household shrank even more when, in 1895, Marguerite married a Swiss doctor, Edmund de Rham. Henrietta Thomasett was no doubt consoled by the fact that Ada and Harold Gripper were living in Khartoum Villa in nearby Grosvenor Road.

To return to Manor House. The last owner of the property was George Bird, a horticultural hybridist of great achievements whose collection of orchids was so large and important that on his death in 1927, a three-day sale was necessary to dispose of the collection. It was entirely appropriate that George Bird should be President of the West Wickham Horticultural & Cottage Gardener's Society, whose annual shows were held in the grounds of Manor House. The shows not only featured produce but also needlework, cooked dishes and decorated prams. A sports programme was also part of the proceedings with a Brass Band, usually Wickham's own Brass Band, providing music at intervals.

Decorated prams at the Flower Show

93

The Annual Show was one of the highlights of the summer in West Wickham. The *Bromley Record* reported on the 1906 Show. "The floral and horticultural exhibits were contained in one large marquee. Right opposite the entrance was a fine group of hydrangeas, the base being surrounded by gloxinias and maidenhair fern . . . The ladies entered largely for the dinner table decorations, in which there were two classes, one for the ladies of the parish and another for cottagers and domestic servants . . . During the afternoon and evening some sports were held for boys and girls and adults . . . a costume cricket match . . . cocoanut shie and donkey rides . . . The Shirley School Band . . . In the evening dancing was indulged in . . ."

George Bird was an enthusiastic cricketer and ran his own team. Another of his interests was butterflies and his collection was presented to Marlborough College. George and Kitty Bird had a family of three sons and two daughters — George, Ryder, Edmund, Margaret and Catherine. Mrs. Kitty Bird died in 1912 and so was spared the worry and agonies of the First World War in which all three of her sons enlisted in the Armed Forces. George jnr., an artist by profession, did apply for exemption on conscientious grounds, but as he was prepared to serve as a non-combatant, was passed for service in the Artists' Rifles. Ryder had a short but adventurous Service career, first as a Lieutenant in the Kings Royal Rifle Corps, then as a Pilot in the Royal Flying Corps. On

Sherwood Court — site of Manor House *Joyce Walker*

a flight over the North Sea he found himself lost in fog with a leaking petrol tank but managed to stay in the air until he spotted a Dutch trawler whereupon he landed on the sea to within 25 yards of the trawler. Ryder was rescued and interned as a shipwrecked mariner, but was repatriated and he returned to the King's Royal Rifle Corps. Sadly Ryder Bird was killed in Flanders in October 1915 and is named on the Menin Gate Memorial. The third of the brothers, Edmund, survived the War serving as a Sub Lieutenant in the Royal Naval Air Service. He died at Keston in 1979.

George Bird snr., who married, as second wife, Miss Helen Packe in 1916, died in 1927 after which Manor House and its grounds were sold for redevelopment, the house being demolished in 1928. Reminders of what once was are the appropriately named roads on the estate and a flourishing holm oak tree at the rear of houses in Manor Park Road.

Oak Gate

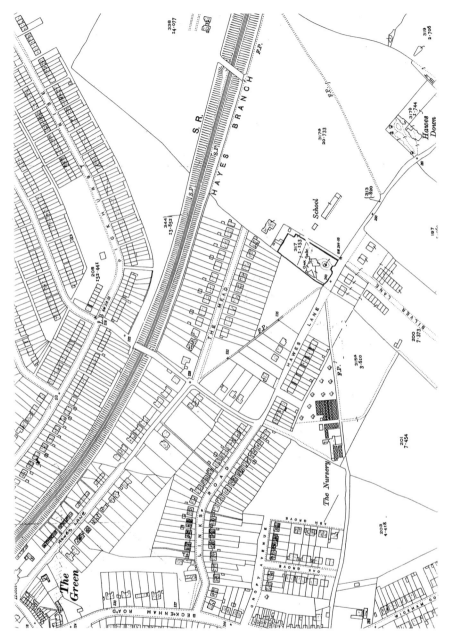

V — Oak Gate and surrounding area c1933

Oak Gate

Oak Gate, so-named because of the old oak tree at its front gate, was situated in Hawes Lane, its site now developed as Martins Close. It was built at the end of the 19th century for Miss Julia Lennard, the unmarried daughter of Sir John Lennard, then Lord of the Manor of West Wickham, following his marriage to Miss Isabella Brand in 1890. Julia, born in 1853, and whose mother Julia died in 1888, was a twin but Eleanor her sister died as a baby.

Oak Gate 1936   *Kathleen Arnott*

Julia Lennard featured in Emily and Ellen Hall's diaries, albeit in acerbic terms, but worth repeating:-

7 November 1884:   "Dear Ellen invited to attend a Parish meeting — found half a dozen ladies and Miss Lennard — who with the Rector, settled every question — Miss Lennard did — not the half dozen . . . There are 250 children!!! each one to have a toy! besides cake and tea!"

29 June 1885: [Emily] "Miss Julia has it all her own way now and rules the rector [Ythil Barrington] entirely — in short it is a close Borough of the olden times — Colonel Sir John, his daughter — his nephew and his tenants forming the vestry and doing just as they like on the school committee."

17 October 1885: [Ellen after evening service at the parish church] ". . . the singing was as loud and bawling as it used to be in Miss Julia's time before. She plays the Organ in the morning at the parish church and in the evenings at the Mission Church."

3 October 1886: [Emily] "Having heard that Lady Lennard is very ill I stopped 'old Juley', swinging home, without gloves, from playing the harmonium in the Mission Church. She is not an attractive young lady! She smiled, a sort of mechanical smile, 'Better thanks' (a word I abhor) 'But we keep her quiet' 'Oh yes, she drives out every day, but we dont let her see anyone except very intimate friends . . . it has been a slight stroke of paralysis — a very lethargic state of the brain.'"

Julia Lennard lived a quiet simple life at Oak Gate, serving the village as befitted a daughter of the Lord of the Manor. She was the honorary organist and choir mistress of the choir at the village church opposite The Wheatsheaf for eighteen years, retiring in 1903. Julia Lennard was also the first editor of the parish magazine when it was inaugurated

Julia Lennard with NAZLI *Mary Hogg*

in 1885, a position she held for a number of years. One of her faithful and long-serving servants was her gardener, Ben Beckingham, also the parish clerk, who lived at Oak Gate Cottage after it was built in 1903.

Gardener Ben Beckingham *Mary Hogg*

Another of Julia Lennard's companions at Oak Gate was NAZLI, a donkey, said to have been in Queen Victoria's service and given to one of the Lennards as a gift.

After Julia Lennard's death in 1924 at the age of 71, Oak Gate was taken by a solicitor, Henry Stinson, a holder of the Military Cross, and sometime chairman of the West Wickham Parish Council.

William Coulson, a professional photographer, took up residence in 1934. He was also inventor of various mechanical objects and, notably, of the country's first portable electric torch powered by a small accumulator, which was used in the First World War by the London police force. William Coulson was a staunch Methodist and a founder member of the Hawes Lane church when it opened in 1935.

William and Mabel, his wife, had four children — Myrtle, Kathleen, Kenneth and Eric. Myrtle, the elder daughter, had the distinction of being the first bride married in the new Methodist church when, in 1937, she wed Sydney Fox, the organist at the church. Sadly, as a Pilot Officer serving in 460 Squadron, Sydney Fox was killed in action in 1943. Kathleen scored another 'first' for the Coulson family when she became the first missionary sent out from the Hawes Lane Methodist Church. Ibadan in Western Nigeria was her destination when she sailed in May 1939. Kenneth, a schoolteacher, served in the RAF during the War. He married Una Merchant and, by a quirk of fate their daughter Gillian, who married a Methodist minister, the Revd. David Curtis, found herself in West Wickham in the 1980s at the very church where her grandfather had been a founder member. Eric was a banker before and after the War during which he served in R.E.M.E.

Kathleen Arnott (nee Coulson) has happy memories of Oak Gate and special ones of the garden. "The garden, measuring almost one acre . . . beautifully landscaped . . . On the northern side was a large square lawn with a bed of tall pampas grasses in its centre and flowering trees and bushes on the three outer sides. . . running down the whole length of the garden was an avenue of chestnut trees which had been part of the tradesmen's entrance, but which the Coulsons called 'Lovers' Walk' . . . close behind the house was a long lawn with a row of tall wooden posts carrying looped chains which supported American Pillar climbing roses. A smaller lawn on the southern side . . . had several beds containing Dorothy Perkins roses trained over domed metal frames, and with miniature bushes of French lilac close by." The garden was also used for church fetes, garden parties and outdoor Sunday School activities.

William Coulson died of pneumonia in 1943. Three years later Oak Gate was sold and by 1962 the house had been demolished and Martins Close came into being. Oak Gate Cottage still remains.

Martins Close 1994 *Joyce Walker*

Oak Lodge

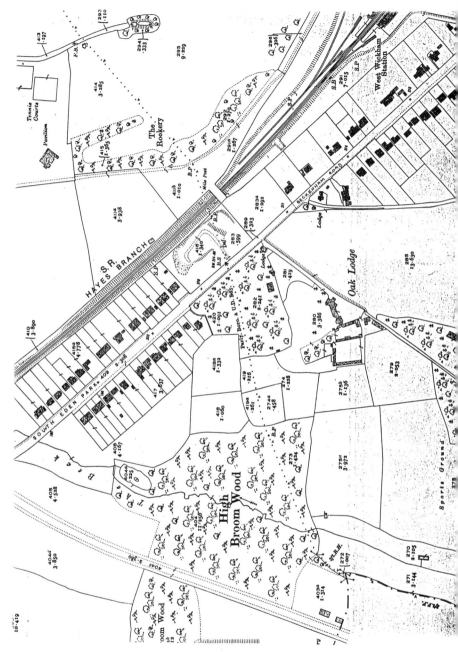

VI — Oak Lodge and surrounding area c1930

106

Oak Lodge

Flanking Blake Recreation Ground in Beckenham Road is Oak Lodge in Oak Lodge Drive. Oak Lodge has not actually 'vanished' but it has been altered and so qualifies for inclusion in this book.

When Lord Gwydir (formerly Peter Burrell) died in 1820 owning most of the land 'above the hill' in West Wickham, his estates were broken up and sold off in lots, one of which was Ridle Meadow. Oak Lodge was built soon after on one half of Ridle Meadow. It was described in the 1970s as a two-storey yellow brick house with a centre front and projecting wings. It had a slate roof and eaves cornice; ten windows, mainly 19th century sashes but two on each side were three-light oriels. The left side ground floor had one large window of eight lights. The right side ground floor had a five-light bow window. There was a

Wickham Hatch/Oak Lodge *Patricia Knowlden*

porch with a semi-circular glass verandah supported by two wooden posts and wrought iron brackets over the front door.

John Wilson Davis, born at Deptford in 1773, was the first owner of the house, then known as Wickham Hatch. John Davis, described in the 1841 census as a grocer, was widowed some time before 1851 at which time Wickham Hatch had been renamed Oak Lodge and he was described as a "farmer and occupier of property of 70 acres employing five labourers". In 1854 Edward Gripper, Emma his wife, and their five children, three boys and two girls, took up residence at Oak Lodge. Another son, Ernest, made his appearance in 1856. All four sons followed their father into the corn-broking trade; three married local girls and settled down in West Wickham. The two girls, Ada and Rose, never married and they too set up house in West Wickham, in the Nest in Grosvenor Road. The young Grippers were very active socially in West Wickham, both in doing good works and prominent in the local dramatic society. For a time the short hill in South Eden Park Road was known as Grippers Hill.

Emma Gripper died in 1889. Edward Gripper died one year later. Both have memorial windows, designed by Herbert Bryans, in the porch of the parish church,

E. Fyffe, he of the banana Fyffes, then took up residence at Oak Lodge for three years. In 1904 William Shoebridge was the occupier. Then came Ernest Bliss who lived at Oak Lodge for seven years. His son William served in the Royal Garrison Artillery during the First World War.

Lodge to Oak Lodge

In 1913 Mortimer Justin brought his family to Oak Lodge, renting the property until 1916 when he purchased the house and its estate in the name of his married daughter, Mrs. Winifred Schove. Mortimer Justin died in 1924, his widow Louise Justin staying on at Oak Lodge. Justin Field, part of the Oak Lodge estate was sold to the Beckenham Urban District Council for use as a recreation ground which was opened in 1932 and named Blake Recreation Ground after Dr. William Blake, the village doctor.

Mrs. Winifred Schove, who, with her husband Arnold, lived at Oak Lodge, allowed the pupils at St. David's College, then centred at 29 South Eden Park Road, to use a field on the estate, shared in the 1930s with a herd of Jersey cows. During the 1930s Oak Lodge was further enlarged, a garden room, conservatory and billiards room among the improvements.

During the Second World War Oak Lodge was given over for occasional use by the pupils of St. David's College. This was because the vagaries of war had forced the College to accept pupils of all ages who, for whatever reason, needed to maintain their studies. Derek Schove, Arnold's son and principal of the College, taught the older students mathematics and physics until he enlisted in the RAF as a meteorologist. His sister, Mrs. Betty Ramsden, became acting principal of St. David's College until her brother's return to Civvy Street. Arnold Schove left

Oak Lodge 1994

Oak Lodge after the War. Mrs. Louise Justin and other members of the Schove family continued in residence until 1964, when the last of the family to live there, Miss Joy Schove moved out.

Oak Lodge, inherited by Derk Schove in 1977, then stood empty for some time, and the house and outbuildings fell into a state of disrepair. In 1988 plans to convert Oak Lodge into 28 sheltered flats, to demolish the outbuildings and replace them with a two-storey block of flats, and to erect a second block of flats in the grounds, were rejected by Bromley Council. But now, with advice from English Heritage, Oak Lodge, a Grade 2 listed building, has been converted into spacious elegant apartments. Some of the outbuildings have also been upgraded into elegant living quarters.

Pond House

Pond House

Pond House was once an old coaching inn, known as the Kings Arms, on the outskirts of West Wickham at the western end of the High Street, accessed by a little bridge over the River Beck. In 1753 the Kings Arms was licensed to John Wicker and from 1755 to 1757, to Francis Norris. James Alexander came next and presided over the inn for 40 years during which period he served as a churchwarden and an overseer of the poor. James was married to Lucy by whom he had four sons. In 1784 the tenants of the manor of West Wickham were regaled to dinner at the King's Arms at a cost of £5.10.7½d. James Alexander died in 1797, Lucy two years later.

The Licensed Victuallers' Registers list one John Burlington as licensee in 1803, the year in which he was also registered as a Special Constable. John Burlington, in concert with other Special Constables in West Wickham — Francis Berrington, publican at The Swan; Cass Townsend, farmer; John Bargrove, shopkeeper; John Cooper, farmer; John Alexander (one of James' sons), carpenter; Thomas Kemp, butcher; and William Whitmore, gentleman, of Grove House; — were required to swear on oath that each of them did "sincerely promise and swear that in the event of the enemies of this country putting to sea for the purpose of invading it, or of actual invasion, . . . will faithfully execute the office of Special Constable for the County of Kent."

Other snippets of information concerning John Burlington appear in Wickham's poor-rate books.

"1812

23 Dec: To pd. Burlington for expenses incurred by
Jas Evans being sick at their house.   10s.4d.

1813

30 Apr: Pd. Burlington for Beer to bricklayers at
the poor-houses   5/-"

John Burlington was married to Sarah. The marriage produced Percy (1806), Selina (1807), John (1809), William (1812) and Eliza (1813).

Two other children are mentioned in Dr. Ilott's Prescription Book: Anna and Hannah. John Burlington continued as licensee at the Kings Arms until at least 1816, the last entry made in the Licensed Victuallers' Registers for the inn.

In 1821 Edward Little acquired the Kings Arms for his own private use, renaming the house Pond House. The licence then passed to a weather-boarded beerhouse built on adjacent land — the White Hart. This White Hart beerhouse was replaced in 1908/9 by the White Hart which stands to this day.

Edward Little died in 1830 after which event Pond House passed to his brother William who was a tailor with premises in Vauxhall. Pond House's postal address was then 1 Park Lane. Following William's death in 1863 Pond House was purchased, at auction, for £1,130 by Lewis Loyd who owned large areas of land in the immediate vicinity.

Pond House was described in the Sale Particulars thus:-

"WEST WICKHAM, KENT

ABOUT 3 miles FROM THE
BECKENHAM, NORWOOD JUNCTION & CROYDON
RAILWAY STATIONS

PARTICULARS

A Compact Freehold Estate

SITUATE AT THE WESTERN ENTRANCE OF THE RURAL
VILLAGE OF WEST WICKHAM

COMPRISING A
DETACHED COTTAGE RESIDENCE
Containing 4 Bed Rooms, 2 other Rooms, approached
by a separate Staircase, 2 Parlours with Bow
Windows, Kitchen, Scullery with Pump, Pantry,
2 Store Rooms and Cellar,

A 2-STOREY STABLE BUILDING
Comprising Stalls for 2 Horses with Loft Over, Chaise House,
Cart Lodge, Poultry, Knife and Tool Sheds.

GARDEN & ORCHARD
STOCKED WITH THRIVING FRUIT TREES
&
CAPITAL MEADOW LAND
Containing Altogether
An Area of 2a 0r 29p, (More or less)

Abutting Southward upon the High Road leading from Croydon to the Village and Eastward partly upon a Road [Park Lane] dividing the Property from Monks Orchard Estate.

The Property is in the occupation of the representatives of the late Mr. William Little and is sold subject to such Rights of Way and Easements (if any) as now legally exist.

THE FIXTURES & IRON HURDLES WILL BE INCLUDED IN THE SALE. The Vendor reserves the right to remove the crop of Fruit and to sell the effects by auction upon the Property.

TO BE SOLD BY AUCTION
By MESSRS BLAKE
At Garraways Coffee House, Church Alley, Cornhill
On Wednesday 16 September 1863 at 12 o'clock"

Tenants thereafter were W. H. Canly (1864-1867), Henry Faithful, a stationer (1870-1871), and William Weymouth (1874-?). In 1877 56-year-old Charles Moule, a tailor/outfitter with premises at Camberwell Green, took up residence together with wife Emily and baby Fanny. Another daughter, Victoria, arrived two years later. Charles Moule died in 1896, his wife Emily, 25 years his junior, died in 1908 aged 63. A year later, Fanny and Victoria, known as 'Pommie' and 'Birdie', moved to a new house in Hawes Lane — The Hollies — where an elderly aunt, Sarah May, kept them company.

Pond House   *Bromley Central Library*

Pond House then featured in the *West Wickham Parish Magazine* when the new tenant, a Miss Tennant, announced that she was prepared to accept pupils for tuition in the mornings. Other names flit through the records:– 1913, E. G. Steele, a poultry farmer; 1916, David Rose; 1918, F. Broomfield; 1921, H. J. Moule; and in 1922, Frank Kirby.

In 1922 the Monks Orchard Estate, of which Pond House was a part, was broken up and sold.

Pond House could now boast that it was within twenty minutes walk of West Wickham Station and that buses passed the property. The two parlours had become a dining-room and a drawing-room.

"GROUND FLOOR —

ENTRANCE HALL; DINING ROOM 11ft x 15ft, into bay, with fitted stove and cupboard, door communicating with DRAWING ROOM, 15ft-6 x 15ft-3, with bay, fitted stove and corner cupboard; MORNING ROOM, with fitted stove.

DOMESTIC OFFICE — KITCHEN, with closed range, fitted dresser and shelves; SCULLERY, fitted sink (h. and c.) and copper; PANTRY; COAL STORE; W.C.; STORE ROOM. In the Basement are large cellars.

FIRST FLOOR is reached by the Principal Staircase and a Secondary Staircase.

FIVE BED ROOMS, measuring 16ft-6 x 13ft, 13ft-6 x 13ft-6, 13ft x 12ft-9, 15ft x 10ft, 11ft x 9ft-3, respectively four of which are fitted with suitable stoves and two with hanging cupboards; BATH ROOM, fitted with bath (h. and c.), lavatory basin (h. and c.) and large linen cupboard.

STABLING
Of Coach House, Two-Stall Stable, Loose Box and Three other Sheds.

Range of Five Pigstyes

The Residence has Company's Water and Gas and Cesspool Drainage installed on modern principles.

DETACHED COTTAGE
Brick Built with Tiled Roof, containing Four Rooms, W.C., Outside Wash-house and Sheds. Well Water. Let upon a weekly tenancy at 10/10 per week (landlord paying rates and taxes), thus giving a Gross Rental of £28.3s.4d. per annum.

116

THE GROUNDS

Consist of Gardens and Grass Lands, the whole extending to an area of over 2½ Acres.

There is a Right-of Way for all purposes along the Road which adjoins the Property on the West Side."

Pond House was purchased at the London Auction Mart by a solicitor, Cecil Austen, who proceeded to alter and add to the house which then had a postal address in Durlings Lane. Two years later Cecil Austen died, his widow leaving the district in 1930. In that same year Pond House was leased for three years to the West Wickham Boys Club, but only one year had elapsed before the Boys Club had to find new premises (at Emmanuel Church) to make way for a new owner — Major William A. C. Denny OBE, a Freeman and Liveryman of the City of London. William Denny's daughter was Joan, wife and cousin of the rector of the parish of West Wickham, Sir Henry Denny. The fact that William and Joan Denny were direct descendants of Sir Henry Heydon, the Lord of the Manor of West Wickham in 1469, was no doubt a source of delight for Sir Henry Denny, a keen genealogist and one-time editor of the *Genealogist Magazine.*

In 1938 Pond House lowered its sights somewhat when it became the offices of D. S. G. Builders Ltd. Adolf Hitler heaped on the final indignity in 1944 when a flying-bomb badly damaged the house which was demolished in 1946. Crittenden Lodge and the Caravan Park in Pond Cottage Lane have taken the place of Pond House.

Crittenden Lodge on site of Pond House   *Joyce Walker*

Red Lodge

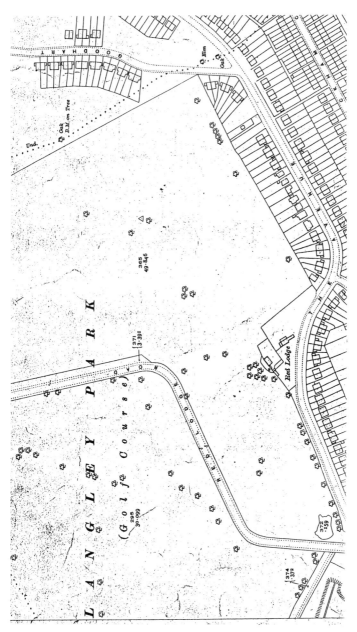

VII — Red Lodge and surrounding area c1930

120

Red Lodge

Red Lodge was the name given to a small house which occupied a site in the fields near Wickham Green on the borders of the Langley Estate — the Frithwood of medieval times — which belonged to the manor of West Wickham. Translated into 20th century parlance, that means a site to the north of St. Mary's church in The Avenue and in the garden of St. Mary's vicarage.

When Lord Gwydir, owner of the Langley Estate, died in 1820 his estates were broken up and sold at auction. The sale catalogue of the Langley Estate contained "Lot 1, Pt. Item 322, Gamekeeper's House, Yard and Garden 1a 0r 35p", in fact, Red Lodge. It was purchased, together with Langley House, by Emmanuel Goodhart. The Goodhart family occupied Langley House until 1903 when the then owner, Charles Goodhart, died and left the property to seven heirs, none of whom was

Red Lodge

inclined to live there. The reason? Because London was rapidly encroaching on the neighbourhood. In 1910 Langley House became the clubhouse for the new Langley Park Golf Club. Red Lodge continued life as a farmhouse where Victor Stock was the tenant farmer in 1921. Gordon Maxwell wrote *The Fringe of London* (1925) in which he mourned the passing of the Langley Estate. "Another of the big country estates that lie on the Kentish fringe of London is in its death throes, its throat being cut by the housing shortage. This is Langley Park, Beckenham, and although but 12 miles from the heart of London, anyone wandering there today will still be in the heart of the country. Fine old trees, pleasant meadows, ponds half-hidden amongst the greenery, and woodland groves, are all that meet the eye of the rambler, over what is certainly one of the finest estates in the Home Counties."

Gordon Maxwell also wrote about the Bath House which Emily Hall of Ravenswood had visited in 1877. "The Bath House, about a quarter of a mile from the site of the mansion, is also worth inspection. Here is a stone-built bath, after the Roman fashion, fed with spring water. Close by are the remains of the old Ice House where ice from the ponds was stored underground for use in summer."

Gordon Maxwell continued — "A small farm — Red Lodge Farm — near the Venison House, [referred to earlier in the text as a "memory of the days . . . when Langley Park was one of the finest deer-parks round London"] is a delightfully picturesque little place, whose farm-yards extend to the woodlands that cloak one end of the estate. By the courtesy of the bailiff I was able to inspect the farm-house. Some of the upper rooms contain some very fine 16th century oak panelling, which proves this house to be the oldest existing building on the estate. It is a charming little place, which I sincerely hope will be left with enough land to preserve its quaint beauty."

Sadly that wish was not to be fulfilled for Red Lodge was sold soon after. The ancient oak panelling was offered to a granddaughter of Charles Goodhart, Mrs. Frederick McCormack-Goodhart, of Langley Park, Maryland, U.S.A., but she was obliged to decline the offer not having the appropriate space in which to erect the panelling. It was sold in 1928 to E. H. Budd of Reading who, in turn, sold it to Acton Surgey Ltd. The Pennsylvania Museum of Art (now the Philadelphia Museum of Art) was able, with finance provided by an American, William L. McLean, to acquire the panelling which is now on display in the museum.

The Revd. Sir Henry Denny, rector of St. John the Baptist church, West Wickham, inspected the oak panels before they were removed. He wrote to the *Beckenham Journal* on 15 September 1928: "They cover the walls of an upper room and are evidently in their original condition

. . . The date 1529 appears repeatedly as do the following badges, the Tudor Rose, the Prince of Wales feathers, the fleur-de-lis of France and the pomegranates of Aragon — but I could discover no armorial bearings. Round Medallions bear heads, some of which may be portraits of Royal personages."

The *Pennsylvania Museum Bulletin of November 1936* elaborated: "The panels which form the Wainscot have each a wreathed branded medallion. In the vertical panels this forms the central feature of an arabesque design, with vases, leafy stems, pairs of dolphins, scrolls or cornucopias and occasional birds . . . A further romantic interest is given to the room by the suggestion advanced by the Revd. Sir Henry Denny of West Wickham that it may have served as a trysting place for Henry VIII and Anne Boleyn — the presence on the panelling of the royal badges with absence of private armorial bearings, has been taken to suggest that the house was a royal hunting lodge where the King used to stay on his visits to Wickham Court."

Efforts were made to save Red Lodge and the Revd. Sir Henry Denny argued that it should be scheduled for preservation and used as a local museum. But all to no avail. Red Lodge was demolished sometime between 1947 and 1954.

Wickham Hall

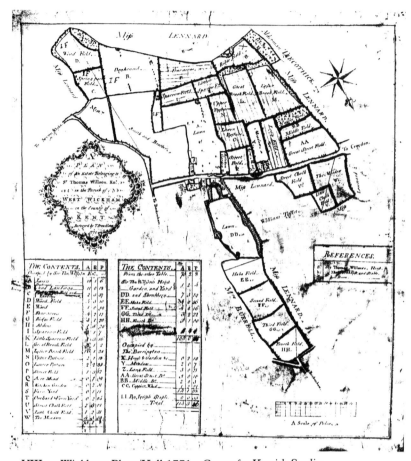

VIII — Wickham Place/Hall 1771   *Centre for Kentish Studies*

Wickham Hall

Wickham Hall was situated on the northern side of the High Street, its frontage, including the stables, extended from Kent Road to just beyond Braemar Gardens. Wickham Hall was built on the site of Carpenters Farm of which there is an estate map in the British Museum. In a rental of 1485 Carpenters was one of six tenements along the road between Norwood Cross (by The Swan public house) and Ridle Lane (say Kent Road).

During the 18th century Carpenter's Farm was gradually built up. One of its owners, Edward Castleford, died without direct heirs and the property was eventually acquired by Thomas Harrison, already the owner of several properties in West Wickham. His son John reversed his father's expansionist policy by selling Carpenters and its land, in about 1750, to Sir Thomas Wilson, who became a Sheriff of Kent in 1760. A new solid red-brick house was erected on the site of Carpenters which, together with its estates, is shown on Map VIII.

Sir Thomas Wilson died in 1775 and, as befitted his station in life, was buried in St. John's church. Lady Elizabeth, his wife, died four years later. Charles Hoskins bought Wickham Place, as it was then known, and he in his turn sold it to Peter Burrell, afterwards created Lord Gwydir.

Tenants thereafter were William Devon (1785–1791), Samuel Farmer (1792–1805) and William Whitmore (1806–1824).

When William Whitmore leased Wickham Hall and its 68-acre estate, the rental was £200 per annum. The new tenant was no stranger to West Wickham having leased Grove House in 'Station Road' for the previous six years. William did have the option of renewing his lease of Grove House but elected instead to move to Wickham Hall which he added to during his tenancy. His wife Eliza had borne John, and twins Sophia and Charlotte while at Grove House. The nursery set was further enlarged at Wickham Hall with the arrival of Charles and James. During the Whitmore occupation of Wickham Hall legal permission was given to divert the southern end of Ridle Lane westwards making use of the land gained for use as a stable block which is now used as a milk depot by Unigate Dairies.

Lord Gwydir, the owner of Wickham Hall, died in 1820 after which time his estates were broken up and auctioned over four days at Garraway's Coffee House. Wickham Hall realised £5,500, paid by its new owner John Howell. After 1839 Wickham Hall was let to a 45-year-old naval officer, Alexander Dixie who was at home on the night of the 1841 census together with his wife Rebecca and their three daughters, Rosamund, Clementine and Emily. As well as the governess, Cordelia Mathew, there were seven indoor servants recorded.

Some short while later Henry Craven, the next owner, took up residence at Wickham Hall with his wife Aurelia and two children, John (1842) and Elizabeth (1843). Henry Craven died quite suddenly in 1845. Emily Hall noted in her diary that she was "much shocked to hear of the sudden death of Mr. Craven — he fell down in a fit in his own room and was dead when she [Aurelia] went in . . . Mr. Cator said he had been drinking all morning and yesterday." The 29-year-old widow stayed on at Wickham Hall until six years later when she married the Revd. William Cator. Emily wrote a tart entry in her diary, "It is strange how the Cators acquire money by their marriages!"

The Revd. William and the new Mrs. Cator did not live at Wickham Hall. Instead the house was let to William Dickenson who, with his family, stayed there for sixteen years. The rental was rather low — £350 per annum but then, according to Emily Hall, "he had to keep it in good repair . . . it was in a sad tumble-down state, unaccommodating."

William Dickenson was also required to maintain what he considered 'parish' drains. He made his objections known to the vestry in 1853. Back came the reply — "The drain in question on Wickham Hall property was formerly a ditch on the west side of the road and the proprietor enclosed it with the waste as frontage and made a barrel drain instead for his own convenience."

Under the terms of Henry Craven's will, Wickham Hall was held by trustees but as William and Aurelia had no desire to live there, permission was given to sell the property. William Dickenson had first refusal but he was unable to raise the £20,000 asking price for the house and its 68-acre estate. William Cator told Emily Hall that Mr. Dickenson, an East Indies merchant, had no money to spare and could not withdraw so large a sum from his own business.

Wickham Hall was bought at the subsequent auction, together with a 12-acre field, by James Staats Forbes, for about £8,250. Emily Hall and other local residents were able to buy up the remainder of the lands. James Forbes was General Manager of the London, Chatham & Dover Railway, with a reputed annual income of £6,000 and so would well afford the expense of such a large house. Indeed he was to spend an estimated £4,000 on improving the house and to indulge his wife Ann and their several children. James Forbes was later appointed Chairman of the L. C. & D. Railway Company and continued its fight against Sir Edward Watkin of the rival South Eastern Railway.

1870 was a time of great upheaval in the education system in England. At that time West Wickham, with a population of around 880, had only a small National School. James Forbes held a meeting to which he invited "everyone who pays rates" in connection with the local school. Emily Hall reported the meeting. "Mr. Forbes mentioned the fact to all of those assembled worthies that there are about 120 children in the parish, only 60 of whom are on the School books and rarely more than 40 attend . . . unless matters are very much improved . . .", he threatened to bring in a school board and inspectors down on them. However, the six months allowed to voluntary societies to make good any shortcomings in accommodation and facilities was enough for the managers of West Wickham's National School to satisfy the authorities that it could meet the requirements of the Elementary Education Act.

December 1870 was a very cold month and on Christmas Day 35 degrees of frost were recorded, resulting in ponds being frozen over and skaters out in force. James Forbes took the opportunity to organise a barbecue on Boxing Day to enliven the proceedings taking place at the White Hart pond. Emily Hall was present, having accepted an invitation from the younger members of the Gripper family to watch

The White Hart 1900

them skating on the pond. She wrote of James Forbes frying sausages over a brazier with accompanying "beautiful floury potatoes and mulled wine" for the guests who were seated on a tarpaulin at the side of the pond, "after which they had hot cups of tea brought from the house."

Emily and Ellen Hall became great friends with James Forbes, but relations with Mrs. Ann Forbes were distinctly cool, as witness many of the pertinent entries in the two sisters' diaries.

In June 1875 Ellen wrote that "he [James Forbes] is getting very anxious to sell the place . . ." In 1876 — "We got a letter this morning from Mr. Forbes offering us his place for £11,000 which sorely tempted Em though I tell her it would ruin us . . . it would be a relief to him to get rid of it as he cannot bear coming down here during the winter." Colonel Lennard did consider buying Wickham Hall but did not proceed.

James Forbes left West Wickham in 1883 and negotiations began with the relevant authorities to let Wickham Hall as a convent. The Established Church was predominant in West Wickham so, when the news leaked out, the rector, Ythil Barrington, made posthaste to London where the Forbes were living, to bring pressure to bear on James Forbes not to proceed with the transaction. It must have been a satisfactory meeting for the convent authorities found the asking price too high. Wickham Hall was eventually let to, and subsequently bought by, Gustave Mellin in 1885. "The people at the Forbes, rich but not educated

Wickham Hall 1897

130

— sell Baby's Food" sniffed Emily Hall. German-born Gustav, full name Johann Carl Gustav, Mellin married an English girl, Emily Bliss, who bore three children — Gustav (1833), Ruby (1885) and Eric (1887).

Gustav Mellin's wealth enabled him to spend a reputed £80,000 on enlarging Wickham Hall to three times its size, based on plans drawn up by the architect Walter Millard. Marble and other materials were imported from Europe and Italian craftsmen were employed on the interior decorations.

Stables at Wickham Hall 1897

Ellen Hall wrote in her diary in October 1892 — "I went round by Mellins, and his new house looks quite gigantic. The part which was the school room is to be built on to join the stable road on one side and the public road on the other — servants' rooms and a ballroom — it will be very ugly and is built of white brick." One wonders what the village people thought of this building, likened to Buckingham Palace, emerging in their High Street. Emily Hall thought the stable block "looked exactly as if he were building them for some cavalry regiment."

131

No expense was spared. The sumptuous living accommodation was supplemented on the ground floor with a billiards room which measured 36 feet by 21 feet with oak parquet flooring and a magnificent Flemish Rococo carved oak archway thirteen feet high and ten feet wide. Other items of note in the billiards room were the set of four carved oak life-size Cupid figures holding floral garlands; fitted electric light with gilt ceiling chains; an ornamental brass 6-light billiards electrolier with brass frame pendants covered with silk rep; 31 panels of embossed Spanish leather; and a massive Bleu Belge marble chimneypiece of architectural design, the top with niche and broken pediment supported by four polished rosso antico marble columns with bases and capitals of statuary marble, enriched with statuary marble carvings of cherubs' heads and scrolls, the centre with a marble bust of a woman on circular socle, shaped mantel shelf and jambs with moulded margins.

The billiards table? That was made by Thurston & Co. Ltd. The table, commissioned in 1893, together with accessories including chairs, tables and turkey rugs, took two years in the making and was delivered in a cart drawn by three horses. The price? £883.16s.0d. It was a full-

Billiards room at Wickham Hall

sized table in wainscot oak fumigated of moresque design with panelled knees, moulded and sunk on eight handsome turned quadruple shafts, moulded bases and carved capitals, panelled sides and eight very handsome carved centres. It was fitted with Penryhn Bangor slate-bed, 'Perfect' low pitch and cold resisting India rubber cushions, West of England cloth to bed and two ring bottomless pockets and leathers.

The playroom on the top floor was more akin to a gallery, measuring 48 feet by 18 feet. The 32 bedrooms were more than adequate to cope with any number of guests, among whom was numbered Bismarck.

Gustav Mellin died in 1902 aged 72. Emily Mellin stayed on in the mansion with her children, one of whom was an adopted daughter, Madge Furrell. Much to Emily's pleasure, Madge married her son Gustav in 1910, making their home not far away in Burrell Mead in Beckenham Road. One year later Eric Mellin married Florence Randall. Both sons joined the Army following the outbreak of war in 1914 — Eric in the Royal West Kent Regiment and Gustav in the 1st Surrey Rifles . There were the grandchildren who stayed at Wickham Hall, no doubt revelling in the delights abounding there.

Emily Mellin died in 1929 aged 67, after which Wickham Hall, the gardens, outbuildings and the kitchen gardens on the opposite side of the High Street, adding up to $10^3/_4$ acres, were sold privately. Some of the contents of the house were sold at auction in the house itself.

Unigate Dairies 1994

There was an auction in September 1929 when the Bleu Belge marble chimneypiece in the billiards room was sold for 70 guineas. The billiards table was disposed of at another auction. Thurstons bid up to 300 guineas but the bidding went beyond that figure and the table was purchased for an unknown sum by a doctor in Eastbourne.

In 1931 Wickham Hall was demolished, shops and houses taking its place. The stables survived and were converted into a milk depot by United Dairies, horses then still being used for milk deliveries. The sale produced a comment in the *Daily Telegraph's* Peterborough column of "Milk to Milk" — an allusion to Mellin's Baby Food and United Dairies. Electrically-driven milk floats now use the spaces once taken by horses. Other parts of the stable complex house a printing firm which has, surely, one of the most interesting skylines of any office block in the neighbourhood.

Now don't I prove it?

This charming little two-year-old girl is evidence indeed for the claims made on behalf of Mellin's Food.

The mother writes:—"Before taking 'Mellin's' she was very thin and small, and the improvement in her health and appearance after a short course of the food was really marvellous."

Where breast milk cannot be given, Fresh Cow's Milk should be modified with Mellin's Food. In this way a food is provided, perfect in nutrition and digestible even from birth

Mellin's Food

A Sample of Mellin's Food and valuable Handbook for Mothers on the Care of Infants, will be sent Free. Write (mentioning this paper.) Address: Sample Dept., MELLIN'S FOOD, Ltd., Peckham; S.E

WICKHAM HALL, *West Wickham,* *KENT.*

5 minutes from Station, 3 miles from Croydon and 27 minutes from London via S. Electric Railway.

CATALOGUE OF SALE

of the whole of the Valuable Interior

FIXTURES AND FITTINGS,

prior to the Demolition of the Mansion, all being of the best quality, with some very valuable carved pieces in Oak and Mahogany, viz :—

FLOORING : 3,000 ft. of Parquet, 4,000 ft. of Pine, 12,000 ft. of Deal, 2,000 ft. of Tile, 2,500 ft. run Skirting and Rail.

DOORS : 140 Oak, Pine and other Single and Double Doors.

WINDOWS : 162 Sash and Casement, 5 Glazed Door Partitions, 21 Baths and Lavatory Fitments,

TWO VERY FINE CARVED OAK STAIRCASES.
A MAGNIFICENT CARVED OAK AND MARBLE ARCHWAY.

Seven Marble Mantelpieces, 9 Overmantels, 38 Tiled and other Fireplaces, 50 Toilet and Domestic Cupboard Fitments. 20 Radiators, 2 Service Lifts, 2 Chubb's Safe Doors, 1,300 Dutch pattern Tiles, quantity of Oak and other Panelling, Glazed Tiling, Electric Light Fittings, Mirrors, Tanks, 2 Ranges

2 HEATING BOILERS, STONE AND MARBLE PAVING, WHITE MARBLE WALL FOUNTAIN. TWO FINE SETS WROUGHT IRON ENTRANCE GATES & PALISADING,

etc., etc., on the premises on

Tuesday and Wednesday, July 29th and 30th,

at **12** o'clock prompt each day, by

HALL, PAIN & FOSTER

Incorporated with

JAMES HARRIS & SON

ON VIEW—3 days prior to Sale.

Solicitor :—
Mr Gerald H. Winnett,
Fareham.

*Auctioneers' Offices :—*48, West Street, Fareham
57, Commercial Road, Portsmouth ; Lavant Street
Petersfield, and Jewry Street, Winchester.

Telephone Nos. : Fareham 14.   Portsmouth 2841.   Petersfield 13.   Winchester 451.

Wickham House

Wickham House

Wickham House, as with Oak Lodge, has not actually 'vanished' but it has been dramatically altered and so is included in this book. 'Wickham House' is situated opposite The Swan public house in the High Street. An earlier Wickham House replaced Crouches, when it would have been described as being situated at the south-west corner of Norwood Cross. (See Map I). This early Wickham House was owned in 1794 by a London tea dealer, John Smith. Then it had two yards; two gardens; two orchards; two barns; four stables; and twenty acres of parkland. In 1807 Wickham House was the property of John Howell who leased it to William Courtenay, the Earl of Devon. During the residence of the Earl of Devon and his wife, Countess Harriet, three of the family were buried in St. John's churchyard:— their only daughter seventeen-year-old Harriet, in 1826; Hugh Courtenay, a one-year-old grandson, in

Wickham House 1994 *Joyce Walker*

1835; and four years later the Countess of Devon herself. The Earl's second son, the Revd. Henry Hugh Courtenay (b. 1811) was curate at Wickham's parish church from 1835–1840 where he had the pleasure of baptising his son Henry in 1836. The Revd. Henry Courtenay's wife was Lady Anna-Maria Leslie, a daughter of the Countess of Rothes. By a strang quirk of fate two of Lady Anne-Maria's sisters had connections with West Wickham. Lady Mary-Elizabeth Leslie married Martin Howorth Esq. and for a while in the 1860s, they stayed at Langley Park and so became part of the local social round. Ever the chronicler of the lords of the manor of West Wickham, Emily Hall recorded a conversation with Lady Mary-Elizabeth who told her "that Colonel Lennard wished to marry her sister Lady Catherine Leslie. She was a lovely engaging person — and they were much attached to one another, but Sir Charles objected on account of her having no money." [Colonel Lennard was, at the time, heir and successor to Sir Charles Farnaby, Lord of the Manor of West Wickham.]

The Earl of Devon gave up the lease of Wickham House in 1843/44 when the Revd. Henry Courtenay was appointed rector at Mamhead in Devon where he served for 32 years. He succeeded to the earldom in 1891.

Wickham House changed hands in 1826 and again during the Earl of Devon's lease when, in 1838, it was sold at auction at Garraway's Coffee House in London. The Sale Particulars described the house as a "Freehold Domain with 90 acres of beautifully featured park-land . . . the principal arrondissement of the much admired village of West Wickham."

In 1848 the Hon. Frances Thomas, a 65-year-old widow, became the owner of Wickham House and took up residence with her three unmarried daughters, Frances, Mary and Albinia. Sometime after that, architect William Teulon was engaged to re-design Wickham House. This he did and the work was completed in 1856. The Thomas ladies moved in the same social circles as Emily and Ellen Hall and so found their way into the Hall diaries. The Hon. Mrs. Thomas died in March 1858 and Ellen paid a call of condolence — "Called yesterday and sat with the poor Thomas' . . . They are going to live in London and will buy a house near to Grosvenor Square. *Miss* Thomas is to buy it." In May Emily wrote — "We were talking of the Thomas's place which is for sale — at not less than £7,000 and as near to £10,000 as they can get . . . my fear is that it may be split up into building leases."

Ellen's fears were abated when William McAdam Steuart entered the lists with his wife and family. On the night of the 1861 census only three of the Steuart family were present:– two unmarried daughters, Catherine (42) and Mary (29), and Adam then 34 years of age. Also

140

present were two grandchildren, Isabella and Maria Steuart.

Wickham House was let for a short term in 1868 to the Trevor family who had hardly been in the house for more than a few hours before an accident occurred reinforcing Emily Hall's reluctance to have gas installed in Ravenswood. It happened on the evening of 1 August. Gas was being installed in Wickham House and the workmen "had left word that nothing was to be touched as the pipes had fresh air in them . . . The footman no sooner found it growing dark than he lighted the gas in the kitchen and in a few minutes there sounded thro' the house an explosion as of a dozen cannon . . . The ceiling of the kitchen was blown up — some of the furniture falling thro' from the room above." The *Bromley Record* reported that because of "the presence of mind and exertions of a few neighbours the fire was extinguished . . . The Bromley and Croydon fire engines were soon upon the spot but happily their services were not required."

During the Steuart's residence at Wickham House, Norman Shaw was commissioned to re-design the house and the work was begun in 1870. Emily Hall "went over to Mr. Steuart's place . . . nearly all of it is coming down. The timbers in many parts are quite rotten and they have found the strangest arrangements — a set of bell wires actually going thro' a chimney which was stuffed with straw . . . Mr. Shaw has persisted in the old site, which is the greatest mistake — seeing that he has more than 70 acres lying in front with a pretty outlook . . ." According to Emily it proved to be a false economy because the original foundations had to be strengthened. Eventually the Steuarts were forced to leave the house for financial reasons. Mrs. Steuart confided to Emily — "We can't save here, and we must save to do up the house and besides the girls' education is becoming expensive." Apparently Mr. Shaw's bill was three times the estimate and so the work was halted. ". . . well may the father of seven children, five of them girls, hesitate and economise."

In 1875 Wickham House was offered for sale at the auction rooms in London's Tokenhouse Yard, with a reserve price set at £40,000 but there was not one single bid. Those present considered that Wickham House was worth only half that figure.

****

Wickham House in 1875, according to the Sale Particulars was a

"Residential Estate about 65 acres in a beautiful and healthy country district consisting of a large modern mansion, suitable for the establishment of a nobleman, or gentleman of position; pleasure grounds and gardens, stabling, cottages and buildings and park-like land, the whole handsomely timbered, part offering magnificent sites for the erection of country seats which will be sold by auction by Messrs. Blake, Son & Haddock at The Mart, Tokenhouse Yard, City on 8 June 1875 in one or four lots.

Lot 1 — A Handsome modern mansion, erected at a great cost within the last five years, under the careful direction of R. Norman Shaw Esq. A.R.A. It presents an excellent example of Domestic Architecture of the period of Queen Anne, combining a handsome and picturesque exterior.

GROUND FLOOR

Entrance under covered porch through two pairs of solid Oak doors into Hall, Corridor and Vestibule together being 90 feet in length. Heated by coils of hot water pipes in ornamental pedestals. An agreeable Promenade in the winter months.

Hall — 19′ x 16′. On left, Ladies Cloak Room 16′ x 13′ having a stove with tiles, side panels and hearth.

Corridor — 44′9″ long

Vestibule 25′9″ x 18′9″ opening from this is

Drawing-room — 45′6″ x 17′9″ finished with handsome cornice, appropriate steel or ormulu stove with porcelain side panels, statuary-marble chimney and tiled hearth. Adjoining is a

Span-roof Conservatory 39′ x 18′ with tessellated floor and heated by hot water. At North end is an artistically arranged Rockwork with Cascade, and planted with luxuriantly-growing Ferns etc. Bay window of drawing-room is in front of Fernery and has a door into Conservatory. Another large window looking into Conservatory opposite Library — 30′6″ x 17′9″ and communicates with drawing-room.

Morning-Room , 18′9″ x 18′

Dining-Room — 26′6″ x 20′6″

Study — 16′3″ x 12′ partly panelled, fitted with book-cases and has French Casement to garden.

142

All rooms overlook gardens and fitted with stoves and chimney-pieces.

Billiards Room 35′6″ x 22′, well-placed and lighted Floor is tiled in centre and in addition to stoves — coil of hot-water pipes — adjoining fitted lavatory and closets.

Principal staircase 5′ wide finished in panelled oak.

1st Chamber Floor — Corridor and Vestibule heated by hot water. Two large airy Chambers 26′9″ x 20′9″ and 22′ x 15′ and five other principal bed-rooms, three dressing-rooms, two Bath Rooms and Closets. (Stoves etc.)

Shut off from Corridor is a large apartment divided into three as Men Servants' Bed Rooms.

Second Staircase from ground to upper chamber floor.

Second Chamber Floor — Twelve apartments — secondary bedrooms, day and night nurseries, school and servants' rooms, fitted with stoves etc. Bath and Box Rooms, Linen Closet and other conveniences. Gas is carried throughout this and principal chamber floor also supplied with hot and cold water.

DOMESTIC OFFICES

Dairy and Larder — tiled floor and walls

Store-Room — scullery with Range, Copper, Sinks with hot and cold and Force Pump from Soft Water tank.

Lofty kitchen 29′ x 17′6″. Benham large range. Smoke Jack. Hot-plate with oven, cooking apparatus etc. Steam cupboard under opening to passage to dining-room, dresser and Housekeeper's room — store closets at sides and enclosed sinks.

Servants' Hall with stove

Knife and Coal Houses and other conveniences

Near Dining-room is Butler's Pantry with Stove, Range and closets, enclosed sinks, cupboards etc. Plate Room with Iron Door.

BASEMENT

Cellars for wine, beer and coals; large Dairy, Lamp Room etc. Furnace for hot water apparatus and Force Pump (Messrs. Owen) which from a Well 40′ in depth, supplies pure water.

OUTBUILDINGS

Stabling of four stalls, loose box, large Coach House, Harness Room, and Rooms over, Cow Houses, Piggeries etc.
Drainage carried in a most complete manner
Pleasure Gardens
Extensive Lawn with picturesque natural dell [now part of a garden in Park Avenue]. Grass Terrace Walk 200 yards in length, shaded with elm, lime, chestnut, yew, holly and portugal laurels and divided from Meadow Land by a Ha-Ha.
Kitchen Gardens — choice Espalier, Standard and Wall Fruit trees, two six-light pits and good water supply.
Meadow and Pasture Land, divided by four with water, brick and tiled Cattle sheds.

28a 2r 16p"

★★★★★★★★★

Wickham House 1875 — facing south

Three years later Wickham House was again put up for auction and it was purchased for the reported sum of £23,000 by Sir John Lennard who resold it in 1881 to Robert McAndrew for £20,500. [Other lots were sold separately] Robert McAndrew was then a 44-year-old merchant and ship-owner, born in Liverpool as was his wife Margaret. Robert McAndrew was not beset with financial problems and so his family was able to live comfortably at Wickham House for 44 years, playing a full part in the social life and charitable works in West Wickham.

One of the McAndrew daughters was Miss Amy McAndrew who was godmother to Mrs. Nellie Willshire (nee Watts), a granddaughter of James Killick the builder. Mrs. Willshire addressed the Hartfield Residents Association in 1976 when she made reference to the McAndrews. "I used to get a very nice Christmas present which was always a delight to receive, and once a year my younger sister and I went there for tea. It was the only time we ever went in the front door and the butler used to let us in, all dressed up in our finery, to go to this afternoon tea. Miss McAndrew would greet us and take us in to see Mrs. McAndrew, a lady I always imagined to be like Queen Victoria, and then we would be taken to have nursery tea . . . It was always after school that we went . . . that nursery tea was soon wolfed away because we were jolly hungry . . . When we had had our tea we would be taken right upstairs to the playroom there but we were never allowed to have a go on anything . . . it was very similar to the one at Wickham Hall. We would just walk along this highly polished floor with all these gorgeous toys and have a look at them, and then walk downstairs and out of the doors into the garden to see the mulberry tree . . . Miss McAndrew always had two tortoises — they were in a pen, quite large tortoises. Then we were taken to the kitchen garden and the gardener there would give us a rhubarb leaf of very very luscious gooseberries and then we came home."

Robert McAndrew J.P. and sometime chairman of the West Wickham Parish Council died in 1902, leaving an estate worth nearly £600,000. Mrs. Margaret McAndrew died in 1925 after which event Wickham House, with 23 acres of land, was sold to a builder, George Spencer, for £10,560. The two McAndrew daughters still at home, Miss Amy and Miss Beatrice, moved to a house built for them in Woodland Way, named Old Field (now enlarged and known as Kathleen Moore Court). A drinking-water fountain was erected in Springpark Woods in memory of Mrs. Margaret McAndrew while a memorial window in the north aisle of St. John's church commemorates Robert McAndrew.

The new owner of Wickham House, George Spencer, proceeded to convert the ground floor of Wickham House into retail shops and to build houses on the remainder of his Wickham House land. He also

145

built shops on the remainder of the High Street frontage i.e. from the Police Office to 'Grabs' on the corner of The Grove. There are those who mourn the fact that a building of such historical significance is caught up in a shopping parade, but there are also those who rejoice that it has survived in part to remind them of an age of elegance and a time when Wickham, was a "much admired village".

Wood Lodge

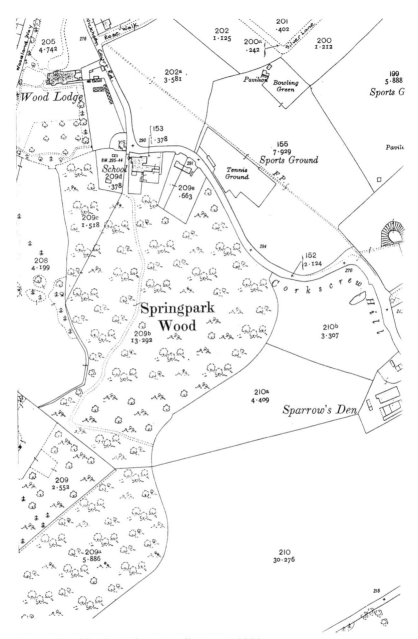

IX — Wood Lodge and surrounding area c1930

Wood Lodge

Wood Lodge was built on land owned by Sir John Lennard, its site now covered by houses in Wickham Court Road, Stambourne Way and Woodland Way. (See Map IX) George Dumbrell, a local bricklayer, told Ellen Hall in September 1886 that "the house the Colonel [Sir John Lennard] is building near the School House is unfinished and

Woodland Way c1930

not very likely to be in a condition to let as for a second time the builder or contractor is bankrupt." It was not until 1891, after Killicks the builders, had "spent . . . a large sum of money, to make Sir John's house more valuable" that Wood Lodge was let to a Scot, David Beath, a merchant and banker. Wood Lodge Cottage (now known as Wood Lodge) housed David Beath's butler, Philip Balsford and his wife Grace and baby Elsie.

David Beath's business interests were mainly in Australia where five of his six children were born. David Beath leased Wood Lodge for three years. He was followed by H. E. Fry; in 1897 Henry Russell, a solicitor and a member of the London County Council; and then Arthur Gurney Preston, a wealthy engineer.

During the First World War, Wood Lodge was offered by its then owner, James Baker, to the British Red Cross Society for use as an auxiliary hospital. The house was prepared for such an eventuality but it was never pressed into service. That War did claim a victim from Wood Lodge. During the Spanish Influenza epidemic of 1918/1919 Mrs. Violet Wigram, wife of the then tenant, the Revd. E. Wigram, succumbed to the virus. Her coffin was borne from Wood Lodge to St. John's church on a wheeled bier.

James Baker was a public-spirited gentleman who filled the office of chairman of the West Wickham Parish Council for nearly ten years.

Wood Lodge

During the economic difficulties that coincided with his period of office, James Baker, in conjunction with the local Community Council, set up a relief scheme to help cases of hardship and to find work for the unemployed.

In 1935 James Baker was desirous of leaving West Wickham and offered Wood Lodge to the Beckenham Borough Council, together with some land, for a nominal sum, for use as a library and park. The Council declined the offer and so James Baker sold Wood Lodge and its 33½ acres of land to Rumph the builders for £24,000. The house was then sold on and it became the Aberdare Memorial Home for Boys.

In 1961 Wood Lodge was demolished and houses took its place. Aberdare Close, Wood Lodge Lane and 'Wood Lodge' serve as reminders of the big house.

Wood Lodge (Cottage) 1994   *Joyce Walker*

Yew Tree Cottage

Yew Tree Cottage

Yew Tree Cottage was an early 18th century weather-boarded cottage opposite The Swan in Station Road, its site at what is now the junction of Station Road and Glebe Way. At one time it formed part of the Ravenswood estate until it was sold in 1922.

In 1888 it was, according to street directories, occupied by G. Welbourne and in 1896 by H. Welbourne a dairyman. In the early 20th century the Yates family came to Yew Tree Cottage which then became a "cyclists' rest" and "Yew Tree Dairy". Then in 1920 a widow, Adelaide Hemming, took over the tenancy and ran Yew Tree Cottage with the assistance of her son Ernest until her death in 1930. Frank Furber took Adelaide's place, and he expanded the confectionery and tobacco side of the business.

The construction of Glebe Way began shortly before the outbreak of war in 1939. This involved the acquisition of land amongst which was the site of Yew Tree Cottage. Negotiations to purchase Yew Tree

Yew Tree Cottage c1935   *Bromley Central Library*

Cottage had begun in early 1938 but were not concluded until 1939. Beckenham Borough Council recommended that after the demolition of Yew Tree Cottage and adjacent buildings had been completed, a "suitable and sufficient area at the western end of surplus land be appropriated for library purposes."

The demolition was to be by means of explosives for demonstration purposes but wiser counsels prevailed and the Home Office decided that Yew Tree Cottage was unsuitable for a training exercise. The cottage was razed to the ground by more orthodox means in August 1939.

The War brought to a halt the construction of Glebe Way and it was not until 1956 that the Glebe Way section between Rose Walk and Station Road was completed.

A surface air raid shelter built on the site was known as Yew Tree air raid shelter. Yew Tree Cottage also gave its name to a British Restaurant opened by the Womens Voluntary Service in empty shops in Glebe Way in 1941. Post-war West Wickham also boasted a Yew Tree Girls Club and a Yew Tree Football Club. Other than these mostly forgotten reminders of Yew Tree Cottage, there is now nothing to prod the memory of this once popular refreshment establishment.

Bibliography

PRIMARY SOURCES

Bromley Central Library — Local Studies Department

Abstract of Title Charles Waller to Freehold Hereditaments at West Wickham
   Ref. 308/1
Beckenham Borough Council Minute Books
Beckenham Urban District Council Minute Books
Bromley Petty Sessions Record Books Ref. 613/1
Bromley Rural District Council Minute Books
Bromley Union Valuation List 1912 Ref. 846 G/By NPa 3/21
Census Returns 1841–1891
Court Baron Records 1749–1899 Ref. 642
Diary of William Emmett Ref. U310/014
Diaries of Ellen Hall 1842–1901 Ref. 855 F/3
Diaries of Emily Hall 1842–1901 Ref. 855 F/2
Diaries of Louisa Hall 1858–1897 Ref. 855 F/1
Dr. Ilott's Prescription Books Ref. 617 1/2/21/23/26
Manor House Sale Particulars 1844 Ref. 907/9/2
Plaza Cinema opening programme Ref. L28.3
Ravenswood Private Hotel brochure Ref. L26.8
Ravenswood Sale Catalogue Ref. 308/1
West Kent Militia & Army Reserve Records Ref. 611
West Wickham Parish Council Minute Books
Wickham House Sale Particulars 1838 Ref. 907/9/6
Wickham House Sale Particulars 1875 Ref. 907/9/1a
Wickham House Sale Particulars 1878 Ref. 907/9/1b

Centre for Kentish Studies at Maidstone

Conveyance of land at West Wickham Ref. U1435/T9B
Copy of will of Dame Mary Farnaby 1815 Ref. U312/T27
Hearth Tax Assessments 1664 Ref. Q/Rth
Land and Window Tax Assessments 1762 Ref. U36/020
Lennard Papers U312/E61
Licensed Victuallers' Registers 1753–1825 Ref. Q/Rlv 4/1
"Messuage called The Grove or Grovelands House" 1715–1759 Ref. U312/
   T2 — 4

Guildhall Library
Annual Register
Gentlemen's Magazine
London Gazette

Newspapers
Beckenham Journal
Beckenham & Penge Advertiser
Beckenham Times
Bromley Chronicle
Bromley Record
The Times
West Wickham & Eden Park & Hayes Journal
West Wickham & Hayes Observer & Times

Public Record Office
Rehausen Domestic Papers Ref. F0 73/76
Will of Gilbert West April 1756 Middlesex 126/822.102.151
Will of Edward Wooding [Wooden] October 1677 355/104

St. John the Baptist church, West Wickham
Church-Rate Book
Directory of Gravestones
Parish Registers
Poor-Rate Books
Vestry Minute Book

Somerset House
Will of Charles Hall died June 1853
Will of Emily Hall died April 1901
Will of Ellen Hall died May 1911
Will of Laurence Sherrard died 1936

Miscellaneous
Returns of Owners of Land Vol 2 England 1873. Eyre & Spottiswoode 1878
Spencer Family Archives
West Wickham Parish Magazine
Wickham College brochure
Wickham Hall Catalogue of Sale 25 September 1929
Wickham Hall Catalogue Sale of Fixtures & Fittings July 1930

SECONDARY SOURCES
Alumni Oxonienses 1715–1886 Parker 1888
Architectural Review Vol II 1902

Stanley Ayling *The Elder Pitt* Collins 1976

T. C. Barker & M. Robbins *History of London Transport* Vol 1 1963

Beckenham Charter Celebrations Committee Official Handbook 1935

J. M. Bellamy & J. Saville eds. *Dictionary of Labour Biography* Vol 1 1978 Reprint 1978

Lewis Blake *Before the War* Lewis Blake 1985

James Boswell *Biography of Samuel Johnson* Dent 1949

Bridget Cherry & Nikolaus Pevsner *The Buildings of England London — 2 — South* Penguin 1983

E. J. Climenson *Elizabeth Montagu* John Murray 1906

George Clinch *Bromley & the Bromley District* 1902

Dictionary of National Biography

David P. French *Minor English Poets 1660–1780* Benjamin Blom

Christopher Harris *West Wickham 1880–1980* Bromley Public Libraries 1983

Malcolm Haslan *Arts and Crafts* Macdonald Orbis 1988

Henry Humpherus *History of the Origin & Progress of the Company of Watermen & Lightermen* Vol III 1874

Alan Jackson *Semi-detached London* George Allen & Unwin 1973

Dr. Samuel Johnson *Lives of the Poets*

Patricia Knowlden & Joyce Walker *West Wickham — Past into Present* Hollies Publications 1986

Sir Tresham Lever *The House of Pitt* John Murray 1947

List of Officers of the Royal Regiment of Artillery from 1716 Edition of 1891

A. R. Mills *The Halls of Ravenswood* Frederick Muller 1967

A. R. Mills *Two Victorian Ladies* Frederick Muller 1969

Michael O'Connor *St. David's College 1926–1976*

Pennsylvania Museum Bulletin Vol 32 No. 172 November 1936

Ravenswood Women's Institute Scrapbook 1956

Andrew Saint *Richard Norman Shaw* Yale University Press 1977

O. A. Sherrard *Life of Chatham* Bodley Head 1952

O. A. Sherrard *Two Victorian Girls* Frederick Muller 1966

Peter Simmons ed. *Hatchments in Britain — Kent, Surrey & Sussex* Phillimore 1985

Francis H. Spicer *Holy Trinity Church, Upper Chelsea 1828–1953* 1956

Street Directories

Canon Thompson *A History of Hayes* Jackdaw Publishing Co. 1978

James Thorne *Handbook to the Environs of London* 1876

G. W. Tookey *History of Red Lodge* 1975

Victoria County History of Wiltshire Vol V Oxford University Press

Edward Walford *Greater London* Cassell & Co. 1898

Joyce Walker *West Wickham and the Great War* Hollies Publications 1988

Joyce Walker *West Wickham in the Second World War* Hollies Publications 1990

Who was Who 1916–1928 Adam & Charles Black 1947

Christopher Wood *Dictionary of Victorian Painters* Antique Collectors' Club 1978

Fred Whyler DFC *Militia. Some Aspects* North-West Kent Family History Journal Vol 4 No. 10 1988

CONVERSATIONS & CORRESPONDENCE WITH:–

Mrs. Kathleen Arnott
Barclays Bank plc
Mr. David Bartholomew
Mrs. Joyce Bateman
Mrs. Amy Church
Mrs. Gillian Curtis
Mrs. Elizabeth Davies
Mrs. Barbro Edwards of the Embassy of Sweden
Mr. J. P. L. Gwynn
Miss Jean Pinnington
Mrs. Betty Ramsden
Mr. Anthony Raven
Mrs. Dariel Raven
Mrs. Shelagh Rogers
Miss Joy Schove
Mr. David Spencer
Mr. George Spencer
Mr. Herbert Spencer
Mrs. Iris Spencer
Mr. John Spencer
Mr. Dean Walker of the Philadelphia Museum of Art
Mr. J. W. Witham

Index